TAKEAWAYS FROM THE
AFRICAN CONTINENT

SHORT STORIES FROM THE EDGE

CHRISTOPHER HIX

Palmetto Publishing Group
Charleston, SC

Takeaways from the African Continent
Copyright © 2018 by Christopher Hix

All rights reserved
No portion of this book may be reproduced, stored in a retrieval system, or transmitted in any form by any means–electronic, mechanical, photocopy, recording, or other–except for brief quotations in printed reviews, without prior permission of the author.

First Edition

Printed in the United States

ISBN-13: 978-1-64111-110-2
ISBN-10: 1-64111-110-0

THE JASMINE REVOLUTION

When there is peace in the country, the chief does not carry a shield.

—*African proverb*

January 14, 2011, started out like many weekend days, with the bright sunlight waking us up around six that morning. The street was busy as people went about getting to work or buying fruits and vegetables for their families. This morning, the schoolchildren played in the streets and life seemed normal—until I turned on the TV to Al Jazeera and started to watch a country begin a revolution in the capital city of Tunis. As the morning progressed, about a hundred thousand or so Tunisians began to meet in the capital, and protesters were asking for the president to leave the country and step down.

As the day went on, the military also began to meet, and they encircled the crowd that was peacefully demonstrating, wanting freedom and change. At two o'clock in the afternoon, the news reported that the president had left the country on his private jet. As his plane went from country to country, from Malta to France to Germany, it was beginning to look like *Where's Waldo?* as he tried to find a place to land his plane. I looked at my wife and wondered where in the world the president would go next. My first reaction was to go to the airport as fast as possible, but it was reported that the military had taken control of the airport and no flights were leaving the country. I called the American embassy and was put on hold and told to call back on Monday—that they were closed. I did not leave a message.

As you can imagine, my world felt like it was getting smaller. Things were changing at such a fast speed that I could not think clearly about what to do. We lived outside of the capital city in a town called La Marsa, where many of the president's homes and assets were located. It was only a matter of time before the fighting would be coming our way. My first reaction from my time and experience in

TAKEAWAYS FROM THE AFRICAN CONTINENT

Kenya during a civil conflict was to fill up the bathtub with water in case they cut the water or power. As I began to fill up the bathtub, my small dog named Fuzi came up to the tub to jump in, thinking she was going to get a bath. Little did she know we were in the middle of a country-wide revolution which would lead to the Arab Spring across North Africa and the Middle East.

I decided to go outside to check out my street, and it was strangely quiet and empty of people. After seeing that many Tunisians were protesting on TV, it seemed they were all in the downtown area of the capital, so I quickly moved my car inside our garage and barricaded the gate, as the protest could possibly spill into the streets in front of our house. The only thought that was running through my mind at this time was to slow all my thoughts down and to listen to the voice of reason, which told me to just prepare for one day; the voice said let's just get through this night and see what happens in the morning. I really wanted to drive to the airport to leave and evacuate the country, but I had to fight off the fear of what might happen in the next few days and try to get things in order at my house.

Fear is truly a killer of the mind and will paralyze any possibility of letting your neighbors help you in a time of trouble. I heard my next-door neighbor getting their house in order while I did the same with mine, like boarding up windows and locking everything down in place. We were shifting now at light speed from a police state of twenty-three years to having lawlessness in a timespan of about three days. I could not travel to Libya or Algeria by land or air, and the airport in

Tunis was closed and military tanks were stationed outside the gates. My neighborhood began to prepare for the worst and for long weeks of looting and lawlessness. We went to bed that night with the sound of helicopters over our house, with a big light that shone down in the street as people moved around with crude weapons in their hands from yard to yard. All night long, we could hear gunshots, and we saw people burning houses in our neighborhood that belonged to family members of the president. As the sun came up, it was clear that the country we had grown to love had changed in a flash. The whole country was put under a country-wide curfew between the hours of 8:00 a.m. and 8:00 p.m. The road in front of my house had been barricaded so that cars could not drive in front of it.

That morning, after looking at the pile of things in our street, my daughter, Hanna, said to me, "I don't think we are going to school on Monday, Daddy." I decided we better go out to pick up some things in the community like food and phone cards and get a look around. The streets were in shambles, and many houses were burned. To my surprise, the bread shops were open, and people were patiently standing in line, waiting for bread. I gathered a few things and quickly returned home, so as not to be noticed by the locals, as they would have noticed an American who had not left the country.

The next morning, after another long night of looting and fighting, we decided to see if we could go out to get a look at what had changed in our neighborhood. My first reaction was one of amazement: On every corner, there were military tanks, and there was barbed wire

TAKEAWAYS FROM THE AFRICAN CONTINENT

around all the banks, and many of the ATMs were burned out and looted. My Tunisian friends were amazed, and to be honest, they did not even know that their country's military had tanks or any kind of weapons like these. We were stopped at every street corner by young boys with baseball bats asking for passports like they had seen on TV in Iraq. They tried to search for weapons like the police had done to them for the many years growing up with a dictator.

As the next few days went on, it was clear that things were in lockdown, as we had no fruits or vegetables. Buses and trucks were no longer in transport. One thing that did become apparent to us was that we were running out of food, and we were now going on two weeks without having been to the grocery store. We needed to eat, but the streets were so chaotic. I decided we had to blend in, find food at our local store, and just buy whatever food stuffs they had to sell. I put on a hat called a fez and a cloak to blend in with the locals.

In Tunisia, almost every family had a store of some kind—either food or a fruit stand. I never understood this concept because it seemed like you could not make any money if everyone was selling the same goods right next to one another. During the revolution, I came to realize why everybody had their own store . . . so they would have food to eat when situations like the current one arose. These stores were symbols of survival, not of making money in the capital sense we know in the West.

I went into one shop and asked the shop owner what he had to sell. In the front of the store, he only had a few cans of beans, but he asked if I wanted to look around in the back of the store. Once I stepped through to the back of his store, I saw he had hundreds of cans of food of any variety you wanted. I bought cans of tomatoes so we could make spaghetti and pasta.

As I stepped out into the street, the contrast struck me in the face. Even though, on the surface, the street seemed chaotic, if you looked closely at each house and at the families who had stores, they all seemed calm instead of nervous.

During that time, we learned to make homemade bread and to cook everything that was in our storage unit—even if it did not make sense. During this revolution, a thriving small economy emerged, and this was special, seeing the local people profit from trickle-down economics. The small shops were all up and running while the big-box store in our town was burned down and sitting dormant like a broken ship. As I tried to slow things down in my mind and take one day at a time—or even one second at a time—I was always brought back to the reality of the situation when my wife, Patty, needed some canned goods because I knew I would have to go out into the community again to find a shop owner who had what we needed to eat for dinner.

Takeaway: Always pay attention to how high your neighbor's walls are being built emotionally and physically, and make sure you have a friend who owns a small food store.

THE KENYAN JOURNEY

There are many colorful flowers on the path of life, but the prettiest have the sharpest thorns.

—*African proverb*

The day was hot and sunny, with temperatures well over one hundred degrees, like most days on the equator. As I entered a big tent along the side of the road that looked like a mirage, one the size you might see in a big-top circus, all I could see was Kenyan men and women standing up, and I was aware that I was the only white person in the place. I sat on a broken, plastic white chair, and as I leaned back, the back of the chair where it was broken pinched my butt. As I turned to catch myself, one of the legs buckled, but a hand from behind me grabbed my arm and helped me stabilize the chair. I noticed that all the people had their heads bowed at this time and their eyes closed.

I took a deep breath and bowed my head as sweat was running down my forehead, and I could feel the warm drops hit my jeans. When I finally got my bearings straight, I heard a loud popping sound which sounded like a loudspeaker, and suddenly, all the people begin praying out loud. The popping sound was mixed with the noise of small African kids running up and down the aisles of the tent, shuffling their feet between rows of chairs that gave the noise a high-pitched tone.

I had never heard or seen anything like this type of worship in a church before, and especially growing up in the southern part of the states called the Bible Belt. One thing was for sure: I did not hear English. My first thought connected with what I had read in a travel book. That in Kenya, over eighty dialects are spoken; I was sure all eighty languages were being spoken or prayed at that moment. As I glanced up, one eye open, I could see and hear people begin dancing on the dirt floors, and it seemed to be a party-like atmosphere.

The sunlight was blurry above my head from the dirt stirred up by the beat of the drums and the stale breeze from outside, and I was feeling light-headed from my blood sugar having dropped due to the heat and not eating anything substantial. I was nervous and scared, and I realized how far away I was from home and from anything that seemed familiar. My thoughts went back to a time when I was twelve years old and spent my first weekend away from my parents with my grandparents.

During the summer months in South Carolina, we all loved to water ski to cool off. On one Sunday afternoon, we went water skiing on a body of water called Lake Hartwell around dusk. As my granddad was pulling the boat around to pick me up to ski, he lost sight of me, and the boat ran over me, just missing my head by inches. As I pushed off the boat, the motor pushed me down with a violent force to the bottom of the lake. As I looked up, all I could see was a white light above me, but I didn't know what it meant. Obviously, I survived the accident, and I am very grateful that such a near-death experience shaped the rest of my adolescent and adult years.

Now, as I sat in the church tent on the south coast of Kenya, I couldn't help but wonder whether the kind of experience I was having at that moment was similar to the one I'd had when I was younger (just without the trauma). As I looked up at the crowd, a hand from behind me reached over and touched my shoulder, and the man said in Swahili, "Karibou," which means "Welcome." He told me that his name was Duncan and that I was in attendance at the largest Baptist church in Kenya, called Ushindi. He said, "Take a deep breath. This service goes on for about four hours, but let's get out of here for a cup of chai [tea with milk] in town while they are all dancing and praying. They will not miss us."

CHRISTOPHER HIX

Takeaway: When heart languages are spoken, listen for the softest one and you will find truth in a whisper.

SAMI

When you follow the path of your father, you learn to walk like him.

—*Ashanti proverb*

This story is about one of the most amazing things I encountered during my time in North Africa. During the summer months, we would have volunteer groups visit us from the States. One time, a family came to visit us, and during their stay in Tunisia, they encountered a young man named Sami who ran a shop and lived in a very conservative part of Tunisia. After returning to the capital, they came by my house and told me I needed to visit this young man; he had such a story to tell, and he needed to see someone who lived in the capital. I decided, after talking with my friend Dave, that I would make the trip south to try to find this guy named Sami.

I had traveled to most of the medinas or open markets in the country of Tunisia. But trying to find one shop owner in a large urban city with huge mazes of shops and restaurants connected to the middle of the city would be difficult. This effort to find Sami would be like trying to find a needle in a haystack. Given that, I set off one weekend with low expectations of finding him. As I entered the outskirts of the medina or open market, the hustle and bustle of all the people began to come into reality. I tried to find a parking space for my car between the carts of goats, horses, and the stands of men selling fruits and vegetables.

Once I parked my car, I knew it might be gone when I got back if the car was not left in the right place or if the police needed money for lunch. Many times, attendants would tell you to park somewhere illegal and then run away.

I entered the medina down a small cobblestone path, with the call to prayer blasting from the low-hanging speakers. I was nervous, as foreigners never went to this particular open market or even this city due to the fundamental flavor of the city, but I had given my word that I would try to find Sami. I must have meandered for about two hours, getting lost and then practicing my Arabic to find my way out of being lost; in the process, I used up all the Arabic words I could remember.

As I was looking for someone to help me find my way out of the maze of people traffic, I noticed a carpet owner who fit the description of Sami standing next to a shop. When I turned the corner, I was then directly in front of the shop, and I could see into the store. I noticed a young man in his thirties sitting behind the counter, reading a book that my friend Dave had given him, a Bible in both Arabic and English. When our eyes met, I knew he was Sami, the young man my friend Dave had mentioned about a week ago.

When we saw each other, Sami ran toward me and hugged me like he had always known me. I noticed that Sami was crying and that he was so excited about me having come to find him and visit. Sami said he had been praying for many years for someone to visit him who would speak the language of the Bible that he was reading. He was overwhelmed with joy that God had answered his prayers after so many years of praying. As we hugged for a moment in the street in front of his shop, as people went by and small kids ran and bumped into our legs, I began to cry as well.

Sami invited me into his office and shop and brought me coffee, which is customary and an Arabic tradition. After talking for a while in Arabic and in English (Sami was very proficient in languages), he invited me to his house for lunch and began to close his shop down. I had never really heard what closing for lunch sounded like, but in the open market, when everybody closes, they pull down these large, steel, rolling doors at the front of each shop. As they're pulling down the doors, you hear this swooshing and cracking all at one time, and it really is scary and loud. It sounds like a plane going overhead. My first thought was about how sounds can have so much meaning behind them for people—and how this sound represented time with family and friends and was almost the sound of freedom for a few hours at home.

Sami asked me to hold his bag while he reached up and grabbed the rolling door. He slammed the door with a force of contentment, as if he were in control of his life, and said, "Let me go by the market to pick up a few things before we go home to my house." The market was full of the midday crowd, and things were crazy, going in and out of shops with all the people hustling and busting to go home for lunch. My mind was swirling, trying to keep up with Sami and his excitement to invite me home. We finally exited the medina, and it felt like I was shot out of a cannon as we came out on the totally opposite side from where I'd entered just a few hours ago.

Sami looked over at me and said, "Let's go in my car. I do not live too far away." I jumped in his car, and we took off down a narrow, winding street to his house. Sami lived in a modest flat/apartment that had two levels and was very spacious—or seemed to have the appearance of being that way due to the lack of furniture inside. I sat down on the sofa next to the kitchen as he began to prepare us a simple dinner of olives, cheese, and bread. His wife and children were out of the house, which I knew was a surprise because usually the women and children are around to visit with sudden guests who happen to come home from lunch.

As I sat next to the kitchen, I could hear the call to prayer echoing off the walls of the house. Sami yelled from the kitchen that we were ready to eat. I moved into the kitchen as Sami was clearing the table of all these souvenirs he'd been selling at his shop. As we sat down, Sami jumped up from the table and said he wanted to show me something before we ate. He had a small balcony attached to his apartment that had a bunch of junk on it, and I watched him go behind a bench, searching for something. He then came rushing back to the table holding a soiled brown bag with something in it. Sami almost tripped coming back into the house in a hurried effort to show me what was in the bag.

As he began opening the bag, it crumpled in his hands from the wear and tear of putting materials in this bag to hide. As he put his hand in the bag, Sami looked at me and began to cry. He said that his wife, who was very fundamental in her faith, had burned most of his religious material apart from this one Bible that he had protected. He'd managed to save a Bible and then hide it from her outside the house. The Bible he showed me was over one hundred years old, which he said a Jesuit priest had given his family many years ago. When Sami was a small child, he had found the Bible one day in his father's library.

As he cried, he said he had been trying to read it for forty years, but the translation was in English. Today, he felt his prayers had been answered. I began to cry as well, as I was totally in the moment with Sami. The joy he had in his heart from a desire he had for so long was now becoming a reality. I looked through the Bible, and it was a beautiful translation. I was reminded that God's word never returns void. I handed the Bible back to Sami. He quickly wrapped it up in the paper sack and immediately took it back outside to its hiding place.

As we had our lunch, Sami began to describe the many dreams he'd had about what churches looked like. He drew graphic outlines on paper to show me what he thought a church would look like if he ever got to see the inside of one. I told Sami that there was a church in the capital city. He looked at me like I was from another world. The capital city was about a four-hour drive from where he lived, and I told him if he ever came to town, I would figure out a way to help him get permission to go into the church to see what it looked like inside.

We finished our lunch, as Sami needed to get back to work, and he was nervous about the possibility of his wife coming home to find uninvited visitors. I told Sami to call me if he ever came my way. This was the start of a very long friendship.

Takeaway: Never give up on your prayers and dreams, and always build a bridge to connect them to reality.

OLD TOWN, MOMBASA KENYA

Be patient with your drum; the night is long.

—*Zimbabwean proverb*

As we walked into the street, all the same noise seemed to be following me from the church. Cars and carts were passing by us, honking horns; people were pushing and shoving; and small kids were everywhere. I happened to step over a dead dog as we were looking for taxis, which are called *matatues*. These taxies are small vans, with many people hanging out of them, and the taxies travel in between the different cities, transporting people the cheapest way possible, in bulk. They are not really concerned with safety.

Duncan, my new friend, motioned for the driver of one van to stop or to at least slow down. You could hear the van a mile away from its music, which had a low, thumping bass. As it approached us, Duncan grabbed my hand, and we jumped into the side door, just missing a large Kenyan woman who was holding a goat and a man who had two chickens sitting in his lap. I was barely hanging on to the van by a rusty door and Duncan's shirt, and three other guys were holding on to me. Every time the van would take a curve, we would almost drop off onto the street.

I could not hear Duncan yelling at me to move into the taxi because of the loud music. The song "No Woman, No Cry" belted out of the van's stereo system so loudly it made the windows shake. My ears were shrilled from the noise. As we approached the Old City quarters in Mombasa center, the landscape and the look of the people really changed, and we had only driven about ten minutes off the mainland from Ushindi on the south coast of Mombasa.

The first thing I noticed about the people walking in the streets was that all the women were dressed in black coverings or veils, which the locals called *bouie-bouies*. To my surprise, all the men had on prayer shawls, and the call to prayer could be heard as it echoed through the streets. It was almost like being in a Middle Eastern country. Duncan yelled over the noise that this section of town was a fundamental stronghold for Muslims on the coast of Kenya. This seemed very strange to me, as I had read that Kenya was 98 percent Christian. Not to mention, just ten minutes before, I'd been in a large Christian church.

TAKEAWAYS FROM THE AFRICAN CONTINENT

How did that demographic change over the years? The island of Mombasa has over three hundred mosques and actually hosts quite a few religions, but Shiite Islam is the strongest, and many of the original settlers migrated from India and Yemen. As we turned the corner for our stop, I saw the biggest red, tattered sign I had ever seen flapping in the breeze from the Indian Ocean. There were words in Arabic on it stating that the last prophet was Mohammed.

As we darted into a rundown shack or lean-to in town, I noticed an old man dressed in a dirty blue burka slumped over in front of a steaming pot of boiling water that sat on a gas stove on the floor. The man looked extremely hot and was shooing off flies with an old, crinkled, yellow newspaper that looked about ten years old. The ceiling fan above his head had only one blade on it, and it was about to fall on him. The flies and gnats enjoyed the swatting game he was playing, and they never really went away.

I learned that flies rest at night in Africa, and that was a good thing, because I think the fly could be Kenya's national bird. The coast was full of them. I would later come to appreciate the flies when I was in Kenya during my shopping trips to the souk because they would help you decide what meat was fresh and what was spoiled, depending on where they landed.

On a table beside the old man in the coffee shop was a set of extremely dirty, random cups in a pink plastic bowl sitting in rancid water. I knew this was not Starbucks and I was not going to see an espresso, much less have my named called out after he'd made the coffee. The old man, without hesitation, poured some coffee into my cup from the previous customer in front of me who'd just returned their cup half full. "No Woman, No Cry," I guess the saying goes.

Duncan motioned for me to sit on the ground, where round, straw mats had been placed to keep from sitting on the dirt floor; the man would bring some chai to us at some point in the conversation. As we sat on the straw mats, I could hear the roaches scurrying away under me so as not to get squashed. As I leaned back on the wall, I could feel the damp, wet, cold wall from the shade of the trees, which felt good on my skin, which had absorbed the hot, dry heat. Duncan explained to me what chai consisted of, and chai is one of the only good things the Brits left in Kenya after their occupation. Duncan looked around to see who was in the place and quietly said to me in a Kenyan-British accent, "What brings you here, all the way to Mombasa, from the States?"

Takeaway: When you go shopping in the market for fresh produce or meat, always look for the food that the flies are landing on—that means the food is fresh.

ELEVEN THOUSAND POLITICAL PARTIES

When two elephants fight, it is the grass that gets trampled.

—*Swahili proverb*

Prior to the revolution in Tunisia, there was a dictator named Ben Ali in charge, and he was the cult of personality for the country for twenty years or so. Because he had a strangle-hold on the people and the political system, there was absolutely no movement in terms of the people ever gaining a voice. After the revolution, all the people began to realize that they could actually protest; they had voices that could be heard, and they could at least assemble and make their request known. Over the weeks following the country's newfound freedom, they began to let people register their voices. I'm not sure of the actual number, but it was reported that around eleven thousand or so applications were filed country-wide, with voices ranging from the Boy Scouts to having a baseball club. This was an incredible renaissance time for the country. The baseball political party was my favorite, and I was able to help the youth in the country set up a productive and functioning program. I spent many years working with the baseball clubs throughout many parts of the country through the Federation of Baseball and Softball. During the revolution, when the fighting had broken out in the rural areas, I would get word from some of my baseball kids that there were many people in the streets protesting. When pictures would come back from the towns, you would always see kids in the streets with baseball catcher's equipment on or holding baseball bats in their hands that I had given out during my visits to the many towns over the years.

The funny thing about baseball in North Africa was the constant clash with soccer, or football, as they call it, because of the teaching structure and the difference between the two sports. Many times, the authorities would call me in and ask me how baseball was played. The police thought baseball was like chess, and they knew that chess taught logical, strategic thoughts. In baseball, to succeed you had to think ahead, and the authorities were worried that the young people in Tunisia would begin to think for themselves and question their rules and their decision-making for their futures.

I would always ask the authorities what made football (soccer) so different from baseball. They always told me that soccer was like a

TAKEAWAYS FROM THE AFRICAN CONTINENT

drug in that it was reactive and you did not have time to think; you were always caught up in emotions. This is how they liked the people to stay: in a state of constant turmoil, the way it is in a soccer match. I often wondered what the authorities thought about baseball after the revolution and seeing all the kids in baseball equipment. I will never know, because the whole police structure to protect the president disappeared after the revolution. The numbers of police who moved back into the civilian population was estimated to be over a million in a country of only nine million.

Takeaway: Never underestimate the power of sports and the impact it can have on young people—especially during a revolution.

THE MOMBASA HIGHWAY, KENYA

Ordinary people are as common as the grass, but good people are dearer than the eye.

—*Nigerian proverb*

The Mombasa highway, or motorway, if it can be called that, meanders through central Kenya down to the Indian Ocean, takes about twelve hours, and runs from the capital of Kenya down to the coast. During the rainy season, the road is washed out and impassable for cars most of the time, and you have to take a plane to get down to the coast.

After arriving in Kenya and coming off the plane, my first glimpse of Kenya was of all the local kids who were lined up along the walls and the tarmac, trying to get a look at all the white tourists or foreigners—called *muzungoos* in Swahili, which means "crazy white wanderers." I think the folklore on the street was that white people looked kind of inside out, and the Kenyans thought the tourists were black on the inside, and vice versa. Makes sense if you have never seen a white person, but maybe a ghost could be dark if it grew up in Kenya.

I was met at the airport by a burly ex-pat named Rusty who was sporting a long beard and wearing those shirts that allow for air to run through when the heat is unbearable (or what you wear when you go on safari). Rusty was my contact person to help me get things settled when I first arrived in country. When I saw him, he said, "Jumbo Chris. Habari Yaku"—in a Kenyan dialect with a southern Georgia accent. The first thing he said was to go get my things; he needed to be at the coast that night, which is about twelve hours away, to see his wife and kids.

As we departed the airport, he told me he had an old used car for me to drive—known in Africa as a "bush taxi"—which was a French Peugeot 204. I realized as I tried to get in on the passenger side of the car that the steering wheel was on the right side, and I noticed that all four tires were of different sizes for some reason. Rusty scratched his head and said something under his breath as he threw my bag in the car: "I thought those guys at the gas station knew what they were doing. It is going to be a long ride home." I had totally forgotten about the Brits driving on the left side of the road. This driving experience was going to be quite different, shifting with my left hand.

As we pulled out onto Ring Road, which connects the airport with Nairobi, I was in total cultural shock, as I had never seen so many cardboard houses in my life, with people taking showers in the street and rows and rows of thatched shacks that seemed to stretch on for miles. I came to realize that Kenya had the largest tent city in the world, with about five million people living in deplorable situations, close to the capital of Nairobi, in cardboard houses called "squatter" neighborhoods. My worldview of a small city life was about to change forever as I drove out of the airport.

As my car entered the highway, the first thing I noticed was a giraffe that was running beside my car, stuck in between two fences, trying to cross the road. It was quite a sight, and I had to stop to take it all in; I had only seen a giraffe in the zoo at home. The only problem was that trucks were heading straight my way, and they had the right of way. The trucks, or "lorries," as they are called, all had the same problem: they all had broken axels, and this made them sway from side to side, which brought them about an inch from the cars as they passed by. I could not even pull onto the side road to get a picture of the animal for fear my car would get hit.

As I cleared the city sprawl and roundabouts, the vast space of the rift valley and the two-lane road seemed to stretch on forever. On a good day, the locals said you could see Mount Kilimanjaro in the distance as you drove down the highway to the coast. The road looked like a dinosaur had taken huge chunks out of highway in sections to eat for lunch. I soon noticed that the shoulders of the road had no shoulders at all with drop-offs of about five to ten inches in some places—which meant that if you swerved off the road, your car would go barreling down the side down the embankment.

    I had been traveling for about two hours with my fingers peeled to the steering wheel when suddenly, a giant lorry swerves into my lane and almost hits my car. I swerved to miss it, but the lip of the road caught my front tire and the drop of pavement threw my car violently off the road. My car began to spin out of control, and my footlockers were bouncing around in the car, from the front to the back seat, like they were fuzzy dice. I ducked down to one side of the steering wheel side as a footlocker went by my head. The car almost turned over as I went headlong into a big acai bush, which is like a tree with sharp thorns on it that resemble knives poking out of it.

    My car finally came to an abrupt stop between two of these acai bushes. A tire had been punctured, and you could hear the high-pitched sound of hissing air going out of it quickly. After all the dust settled, Rusty was nowhere in sight, and all that I could imagine happening at that moment was a tribe of Kenyans surrounding my car and, well, cooking me for dinner. It's crazy what stereotypes come to mind in a cross-cultural setting when people have been influenced by the media and have grown up seeing things on TV or reading frightful stories in books. When you add stress to the event, it is hard not to panic and to remain calm. When I climbed out of passenger-side window to check the damage, it was eerily quiet, and there was absolutely nobody around except for an occasional tumbleweed that would blow by. I knew I had to move quickly if I were to solve the predicament before nightfall.

Of course, the spare tire was another size as well. I quickly changed it and returned to the highway to continue the journey to my new home. This battle of cat and mouse between my car and the lorries went on for about another eight hours as I white-knuckled the drive all the way down to Mombasa. I did not see Rusty again until a week later at a coffee shop in town. I said more prayers on that trip than I ever had before, and I cannot really say how I made it all the way down to the coast.

Takeaway: If you drive a car that has four different tire sizes, make sure the spare tire matches one of them.

ROUND BREAD AND HOUSES UNDERGROUND

A small house will hold a hundred friends.

—*African proverb*

During my time in Tunisia, I had no idea that it was where George Lucas filmed the movie *Star Wars*. Lucas used all the cities and towns in Tunisia for names in his movies. There is a desert town in southern Tunisia called Matamata. This beautiful place was home to the Berbers, the original peoples of North Africa. Berbers are known for living in underground dwellings, with a hole dug out of the top of these houses. You could literally look down into the top of the house.

The connection to *Stars Wars* never really dawned on me until I traveled into southern Tunisia and visited the Berbers in that area.

A local friend told me he wanted to show me something he thought I might find interesting. He said an American guy named George Lucas had come there during the Peace Corps days and had an idea for a movie called *Star Wars*.

As I wandered in and out of the rooms, I was shocked by all the movie props thrown to the side, from the R2D2 model to the bar scene stuff. The Tunisians were still making a small fortune from the tourism trade of Europeans who were interested enough to visit the sites.

From a functional standpoint, the houses were built to trap cool air in, like a refrigerator. The temperature could be well over 110 degrees, but inside the houses, you would need a light jacket to keep the cool out in the early evening. I learned so much from the Berbers as people, and that their lifestyle was from the heart.

The Berbers had survived for thousands of years in the desert, and they were thriving. They taught me how to press couscous, a traditional dish, olives for olive oil, and how to store food in huge clay pots. The days in the desert are long, but the rich family element that they rely on is second to none. The community was at the core of everything they did. At night, they would all come together to visit and sing songs from their oral tradition. The idea for *Stars Wars* was just an idea, or a narrative, that allowed me to go deeper with my Berber friends and really get to know them. One of the most enjoyable things I always looked forward to during my visits was homemade bread. The Berbers had a clay oven that was round like a mound with a

TAKEAWAYS FROM THE AFRICAN CONTINENT

hole in the top of it. They would make a dough ball and then stick the bread to the inside of the oven and cook this under charcoal. They would remove the bread, and it had a wonderful aroma and color, always round and crusty on the outside and soft in the middle.

The Berber culture had been exploited, and not much of the revenue from the *Star Wars* movie had been given back to them in profits. I learned what hospitality was all about, living with the Berbers of North Africa. I made many friends over the years through my travels and was greatly blessed to learn the way of the desert and how to find water through many different pathways.

Takeaway: Bread that is cooked in a round oven will always come out round and cannot be cut into slices but must be eaten with your hands.

"THE CALL" AT MOMBASA HIGH SCHOOL

If you ride a lion, consider how you want to get off.

—*African proverb*

The call of the mosque at five in the morning had stirred me awake for my first day of classes at the high school. The crows in the trees and the water carts would never let you sleep past six on any given morning anyway. The apartment I was living in had no running water, or at least running in the pipes that had been put into the house at one time. The city of Mombasa would ration water most of the time, and usually in the middle of the night, you could hear water going into a tank on top of the house. I would always jump up to either take a shower or wash clothes during that time.

TAKEAWAYS FROM THE AFRICAN CONTINENT

It was crazy, but the whole neighborhood was trapped into a pattern which became a maze of thinking. The whole town would all get a break if the president would come into town because he always wanted people to be happy and to come out to see him, so they would turn on the water early in the evenings upon his arrival. Every month or so, you would get a bill to go pay for your water, even though you may not have even received any water for that month. This experience always intrigued me, as I would stand in line for hours and wonder why we were all doing this useless task.

One day on my way to my classroom, I happened to look up into the sky and noticed a black flying thing coming straight toward me. As I turned to miss it, a huge fruit bat landed on my jeans and was stuck to the fabric with his feet like a Velcro ball. All I could do was look down at his small hairy head looking up at me. I did not panic for some reason, but all the school kids started laughing, and the loudest laugh of all was from Duncan, the assistant headmaster at the school. I gently picked the wings of the bat from my jeans, and he flew away happier than I was. So, I continued on to class, a bit freaked out but happy not to have been bitten.

Our high school was located on Mombasa Island, which was connected to the mainland by a causeway surrounded by water, with over three hundred mosques located on it. To say the least, we could hear the call to prayer five times a day. Many of our students were Muslims who would take off their religious coverings upon entering the school before classes. It was always interesting to see what type of t-shirts the students would have on under these coverings. My favorite ones were of Madonna or a rock band that I am sure no Kenyan would have ever known.

The high school had a religious affiliation, so it was best to have this policy in place for them not to wear religious clothing inside the school. Many of my classes had at least fifty students in them, and it was very crowded most of the time. Many of the students had named themselves after former US presidents, so taking attendance each day was interesting. Outside the classrooms, we always had a gardener who was working in a small garden that had been planted in between the classrooms outside the windows. You would always see corn or tomatoes being grown in season. Just like clockwork, during class, you could hear him singing Christian hymns in Swahili.

The first thing I noticed about the school when I arrived was that there were about ten or so broken lawn mowers just lying around outside the walls of the school, and it always made me wonder why. I asked the headmaster one day about this, and he said the American teachers thought it would be a good idea for the workers at the school to help them cut grass, so they would donate the lawn mowers to the staff. He said the mowers always lasted until the motors broke, and because nobody knew how to fix them, they were thrown into the corner and the workers went back to cutting grass with a *panga* (Swahili word for machete).

TAKEAWAYS FROM THE AFRICAN CONTINENT

Takeaway: If you do not teach people how to do things, they will never learn how to do those things for themselves and will learn helplessness. And always live like the president is about to visit your town or city.

THE BEST THINGS IN LIFE ARE FREE (REVOLUTION BREAD)

An abundance of food at your neighbors' will not satisfy your hunger.

—*Bayake proverb*

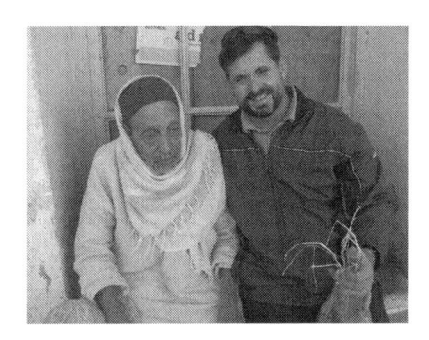

During the revolution, or the Arab Spring, many quirky things would happen for which there would be no explanation. During the martial law period of unrest, we would get extra minutes sent to our phones from outside the country. This was so amazing because the phone systems were so bad, and when the country melted down, it was virtually impossible to get scratch-off phone cards in which to recharge your phone—they had all been stolen. Every so often, during the first days of the revolution, we would receive a two dinar recharge out of the blue, and it was like gold to be able to call people.

TAKEAWAYS FROM THE AFRICAN CONTINENT

Also, during that time, all the bakeries started making bread around the clock to keep up with the demand of the people's needs. They would just give it out for free in the morning and the afternoons. I spent many days enjoying fresh bread and seeing all the people milling around in the streets.

Another funny incident that seemed to happen all the time was that my wife, Patty, would make this chocolate chip cake during the Arab Spring. What started out as a funny thought and was really all we had to eat during the time of unrest in the country became a watershed moment for us and for the dictators in North Africa and the Middle East to be overthrown from power. The first time Patty made the revolution cake, I turned on the TV to Al Jazeera, and over a hundred thousand Tunisians were in the streets, protesting for Ben Ali to leave the country.

Around two in the afternoon, the dictator flew out of the country. The country ransacked his house and his belongings to get revenge. Two weeks later, Patty made the revolution cake again for the kids and Gaddafi came on TV and said that his country was under a revolution and that he and his sons would go into hiding. The next time Patty made the revolution cake, the same thing happened with Mubarak in Egypt. We began to freak out just a little when Patty made the cake once again and Saleh was overthrown in Yemen that same day. As fun as this phenomenon was to track, we decided it may be best to change up the recipe!

CHRISTOPHER HIX

———

Takeaway: When you make revolution cake too many times, the world changes in a mighty way.

EASY LIKE SUNDAY MORNING

To warm oneself is to sit by the embers.

—*Kenyan proverb*

On Sundays, we usually had church at the school and then went out to lunch at a beach club. This Sunday afternoon, I invited a fellow teacher over to have lunch with me. He was the basketball coach, and he wanted me to help him with the team. Anderson was a great person who had a heart for the kids of the coast. He was from the upcountry in Kenya and had come to Mombasa to teach. We had a wonderful time that afternoon, eating and visiting, but little did I know what was about to happen to him the next day.

I could not sleep that night and was restless as the electricity went off and on. When the ceiling fans went off, it was too hot to sleep, and the mosquitoes would start to bite because there was no air circulating.

Early in the morning, my phone rang in my apartment, and a voice on the line said in a panicked tone, "Come to the school office quick! I think something has happened to Anderson." As I hurried over to find out what had happened, all my mind could remember was how peaceful a time we'd had just yesterday at my house.

As I entered the office, the secretary said, "I think someone saw Anderson lying in the street, in a pool of blood, on a busy road close to the school, face-down, not moving." Because I was the only one with a truck, they expected me to try to find out what happened, as I could go quickly to the accident. I was told to go get a white sheet and meet at the front of the school as soon as possible. As I raced to get my truck, many students asked me what had happened, but I told them I did not know for sure.

When we arrived at the scene of the accident, many people were standing around, looking at the car that had hit my friend. One man said he had seen Anderson get off a small bus, and he was crossing the street to the school when another car hit him and threw him onto the hood of a passing car. We asked the people where he was, and we were told that a stranger had picked him up and taken him to a hospital in the city. We loaded up my truck and began the long process of going to every hospital in town to ask about Anderson.

As we went to each hospital in town, nobody had heard of Anderson or the accident. Our last option was to run down to the state hospital close to the school. This was the kind of place where folks were making caskets outside the front door, and the stench of death was in the air. One of the teachers asked a guard if anybody had been brought in so far that day, but he got no response. Another guard told us to stay put for a minute and that he would return shortly with an answer. The guard returned, but I could tell the news was not going to be good or what we wanted to hear. My life changed after I was told Anderson had indeed been brought to their hospital and had passed away.

Takeaway: If a hospital is making coffins outside the front door, find another hospital if you want to live to see another day.

DEATH OF A FRIEND

When there are two people, there is double wisdom.

—Zambian proverb

The guard proceeded to lead us back to a room behind the hospital. The stench of death came out of the front door, which hung by a single hinge. It was hard to see the door, as the Hindu temple adjacent to the hospital was in the process of a cremation. All the smoke was being blown into the morgue by a typical Mombasa wind. I put my hand over my mouth and nose, as the smell was strong. The stench just carried me along. The guard said we could look in the morgue around back if we had time, that a few bodies had been brought in that morning. I realized then why I had been told to bring a white sheet, although it was dripping with sweat by that point, clutched in my hand, and I'd had to use it to wipe the sweat from my face.

TAKEAWAYS FROM THE AFRICAN CONTINENT

As we entered the room, the first thing that caught my attention was two men who were standing over two bodies, clearly in decay. They were sawing off limbs and doing a basic autopsy. I'd stepped over about ten or so bodies when I discovered what looked like my friend Anderson leaning up against the wall, slumped over. It just looked like he was asleep. Once I got closer, I could tell he had taken a significant blow to the head, but the blow did not look life-threatening. He had lost a ton of blood, and it was clear that this may have been the reason for his death. Possibly, he might not have had an insurance card, which would not have allowed a hospital to admit him and stop the bleeding.

One of the teachers grabbed for the white sheet I was holding, but my reflex was to pull against his hand as I gripped it tightly. We wrapped Anderson's body up in the sheet to carry him out of the morgue and then try to find a cold place for his body to stay until we contacted his family. The adventure really began at that point. We placed Anderson in the back of my truck. A few of the teachers got in beside the body, and the sheet was stained red where Anderson had been hit in the head.

We pulled out of the state hospital and started going to different private hospitals in the city, looking for a place to put his body on ice, so to speak. It was very strange to come to a stoplight and have people look at our situation, with the body and all. I could only imagine what people might have thought if I had been doing that in the United States. Every hospital we stopped at was full of bodies, and I was beginning to think that everybody had died that day. This whole situation foreshadowed living in Sub-Saharan Africa; the realities of life that occur every day for them in terms of life and death.

It just didn't look like we would find a place for him until the last place we stopped, where one of the teachers knew someone who worked at the morgue. I'm not really sure what happened, but a body was pulled out of cold storage, so Anderson could be put on ice until his family could make it down to the coast. I took a deep breath, happy that we were able to find a hospital willing to store the body. That experience was the longest day of my life, as we all drove back to the school in complete silence, not really knowing what to say.

Anderson's family was contacted, and they eventually made the trip to the coast to pick up the body. The way they took his body back to the upcountry was quite a sight, as well. When his family arrived for the body, they had rented a van. They put the coffin on top of the van for the long, two-day trip to bury him in his hometown. When the body would smell, they would spray it down with scented spray. I wondered why I'd been so concerned with finding cold storage for him after they told me how they were going to transport him back to the upcountry—but the song "No Woman, No Cry" came back to my mind. As the minivan drove off, they waved goodbye as I turned away from the exhaust of the bus. I never saw his family again.

TAKEAWAYS FROM THE AFRICAN CONTINENT

Takeaway: Never underestimate the power of friendships during a crisis, and always have a clean white sheet around.

REFUGEE CAMPS IN THE DESERT

The surface of the water is beautiful; it is no good to sleep on.

—Ghanaian proverb

A refugee camp started in the strangest place during that Arab Spring. The country of Libya began a revolution which led to overthrowing the dictator Momar Gadhafi. During this time of instability in Libya, about fifty thousand refugees who had been trapped in Libya began to spill over into southern Tunisia, into a town called Ben Guerdane and Tataouine. Most of the refugees in Libya were from Sub-Saharan Africa, India, or Pakistan.

I never thought I would ever see young men from Nepal in Northern Africa. The exodus of refugees out of Libya occurred so fast that they basically ended up in a desert with no running water or food. The first responders to the crisis didn't really know what to do in terms of how to handle the large group. There was no running water at the

TAKEAWAYS FROM THE AFRICAN CONTINENT

sites and no wall or boundary separating the camp from the outside world. I entered the camp from the road, walking through what felt like a semitransparent, invisible membrane that had a different reality attached to it. All the refugees had mattresses on their heads, and tents were stacked together by ethnic or demographic groupings.

The one thought that struck me the most was seeing all the refugees from Pakistan and Nepal standing in an open field, taking a shower with buckets of cold water. All the Nigerians were together, as were the Egyptians, and many other Arabic people from over thirteen countries huddled together.

As I walked through the camp, I saw the word "mujahadeen" written all over the outside of the tents of the people from Somalia. As an American living in North Africa, I knew this word had come to mean to fight and kill Americans at all costs, and walking through the camp was scary. I kept thinking at some point that I would either see George Clooney or Angelina Jolie, but the crisis had happened so fast that they did not have time to respond or raise any money for charities.

I spent the next few days giving out food, packs of crackers, and water to the refugees. I had never seen people standing outside in open fields, semi-clothed, taking showers as they stood alongside one another. Most of the refugees had been standing in line for many long hours waiting for food at the food stations. They were given basic food like crackers, fruit, and a sandwich.

One evening around dusk, as I was helping distribute food for the refugees, the lights that had been set up to work at night had gone out, and we were in complete darkness. I realized quickly that no form of security had been set up in the camp by the military and that I was in a vulnerable place to be as an American. When I had an opportunity, I started to make a run for it out to the street, but a military person grabbed my arm and said I needed to get in line.

After he let go of my shirt, I realized there was a small opening in the line and I could make it to the street if I walked quickly past the guards on the other side because their vision was blocked by a line of refugees. I made it to the road and looked back briefly at the camp as the dust settled. I noticed the lights were coming back on in a staggered fashion, and the shadows looked like heat lightning due to the reflection on the ground and on the people's faces as I left the camp. As I caught my breath, I found a car ride back into town to get a good night's sleep, only to go back the next day.

I will never forget what it felt like to be a refugee, trapped in a feeding station for a brief time. That experience will stay with me forever.

Takeaway: Never look down too long at the ground. The military cannot see your eyes, and they will think you are a refugee—because you are faceless.

THE CITY OF WAR

A chameleon may change its colors, but never its behavior.

—*Tanzanian proverb*

M ombasa, Kenya, was a coastal city that I had not really heard about before traveling to Kenya. I had grown up seeing pictures of Sub-Saharan Africa but did not realize that Mombasa was all Muslim and the rest of Kenya was Christian. This mix of traditional African religions and cultures made it an interesting place to be as all the different religions seemed to coexist or at least stay out of one another's way.

In the city center, you could hear and see a Hari Krishna temple, or a tent with people celebrating Jesus, or a call to prayer at a mosque at any moment throughout your travels in the city. On certain days of the week, you could get dusted by a cremation happening at the

Hindu temple when you walked by if the air was blowing just right. I often wondered if the persons being cremated really wanted their ashes spread on strangers' clothing and shoes to all parts of the town.

One of my favorite places to eat in town was called "the toilet paper roll" by the locals which, by some coincidence, was adjacent to the Hindu temple. This restaurant was a dive that served shaved Turkish meat and kabobs called *shawarma*. The reference to toilet paper in its name was because people always ate with their hands, and the only napkins were toilet paper rolls on the tables. It was quite humorous to roll off a bit of paper, sitting at the table with Kenyans, while the cats ate anything that came off the table under your feet.

My wife, Patty, and I loved going to this place, and toilet paper is now forever in our minds as table napkins. Just thinking about Kenyans passing or throwing the roll to each other during dinner still makes me laugh.

Takeaway: Never underestimate the many uses of toilet paper. From table napkins to coffee filters, it should be treated with the utmost respect.

BASKETBALL AND BARE FEET

By the time the fool has learned the game, the players have dispersed.

—*Ashanti proverb*

After teaching classes in the afternoon, I was assigned the job of coaching basketball. Coaching was not so hard of an assignment; it just seemed so different than what I grew up with in the States. After school one day, I went to look at the basketball courts, and the first thing I noticed was that the basketball rims had no nets attached to them. My first job as coach, I thought, would be to put up nets. This act would make things look better, and the players could shoot with more precision and focus. So, I went about the process of getting nets on the goals. I was so proud, thinking this would help the players shoot better. After warm-ups, nobody was able to make a basket, and the nets were taken down. The Kenyans grew up playing basketball with no basketball nets, so the visual acuity was set differently for them—not to mention the rims had no place on them to attach a net.

One day during practice, my players showed up not wearing any basketball shoes. There is a term for being barefooted in Kenya, which is called "flesh-flops." This is an incredibly hard callous that surrounds the feet of a Kenyan, developed over time when someone does not wear shoes. I felt bad about how the court could be hurting the players' feet, so I went to the souk, or market, to make sure they all had basketball shoes. The idea to buy them shoes did not go over well, so we just put the shoes in a bag for another time, to be used later for tournaments and other things.

One of my fondest memories of my basketball experience in Africa was the time two Masai warriors showed up at my house wanting to play basketball, all dressed in traditional clothing. The two guys were very intimidating in their warrior clothes with all the beaded clothing, not to mention they were about six and a half feet tall and could jump higher than the basketball rims. I asked them to come back to practice after school and we would give them a chance. I had not even begun to figure out how to get them into school because I thought they were about twenty-five years old. It would seem odd to have them in a high school classroom.

As I was standing on the basketball court, the two Maasai warriors marched out onto the court. I placed one of them under the rim and told him I would pass him the ball to shoot the basket. I passed him the ball, but he didn't raise his hands in time to catch it. The even funnier thing, though, was that he jumped so high, he hit his head on the goal, which knocked him out.

After one game during the season, we defeated the opposing team and were chased off the court by bows and arrows and spears (in a polite way). We made it to the bus as the arrows hit the side windows, and we headed back to school. I also had another player named Steve who was from a tribe called the Luo, who decided that if he broke the rims of the other team's goals, we would have to return to our school to play the next game—and it always worked. Without fail, Steve would go up to dunk the ball, and then he would hold on to the rim on the way down, which broke it. He would always say to me, "Hey, Coach, I got this for you to have." In Kenya, most of the rims weren't mounted to the backboards very well, so breaking the rims wasn't too difficult, although Steve was a big Kenyan. After the rim was broken from the backboard, we always went back to our school to finish the game—which gave us the home court advantage—and we usually won the games.

Takeaway: Perceptions can be deceiving. You must adjust your own perspective so you are able to understand other cultures better.

VISIONS AND DREAMS

A person never gets lost among people.

—*Zimbabwean proverb*

One afternoon, I received a call from a friend from the south of Tunisia. I answered the phone, and a loud voice said, "Hello, Chris, this is Sami!" I almost dropped the phone, as I never thought Sami would have a chance to visit the capital city. I had visited Sami at his home many times, but his work schedule always prevented him from having the time to visit. I scrambled to wake up from a brief nap, so I could really listen to him.

I said, "Where are you?"

"Close to the downtown roundabout," he said. He wanted to see the church I'd told him about, to see if his dreams and visions about what a church might look like were true. Just that morning, I was thinking about Sami and his life in the south. I told him I could meet him at the Anglican church in twenty minutes and that he should park in the back of the church and wait for me. I needed to call the pastor because it was Sunday afternoon, so everything was locked up. We would have to go in a side door to make sure we could get in to the sanctuary. Sami hung up quickly after he said he would meet me as soon as possible.

I dressed quickly and started downtown to meet him. I called the pastor of the church and told him the situation, and he agreed to let me into the church. I arrived downtown just in time to see Sami coming up the walkway in front of the church. Sami was already becoming emotional. We greeted the pastor, who unlocked the very big deadbolt. As the chains fell to the ground, it reminded me of my first memory of Sami in the medina, when all the rolling doors were being shut. This time, the doors were being opened for Sami—to a new life.

I rested my hand on Sami's shoulder and asked him if he was ready to go inside. He nodded his head yes. The pastor told me that we could take our time inside and that he would lock up after we left. We gently pushed the huge doors open, and this wonderful fresh air rushed in and struck us on the face as it went out the door. As we entered the sanctuary, Sami said, like a little child, "It looks like my vision in my dreams." We were standing at the back of a long center aisle, and we could see the altar in front of us, which seemed a mile or so away from us.

As I looked around, I noticed Sami was beginning to shake, either from crying or from just being in the moment. Just as I was about to grab him, he dropped to his knees and began sobbing violently, asking for forgiveness. I sat down in the pew beside him and wept with him. Sami began to crawl to the front of the altar on his hands and knees as he continued crying and shaking. I walked behind him quietly, as this was all too much for him to understand and take in.

When he was at the front of the altar, Sami reached up and grabbed a railing that encircled the front. His hands gripped it with so much force, I thought it was going to break. His hands were still shaking, and the rail swayed back and forth. I walked up to Sami and put my hand on his shoulder. He just looked down and would not look up. We both began crying again because the moment was so intimate and special, being in the church under these circumstances.

Sami eventually moved back away from the altar and sat next to me in a pew. We sat another hour or so, quietly looking at all the stained glass inside of the church. Sami looked over at me and said, "The church is more vibrant in person. It is so real, like my dreams. I always knew this existed here. I just never could allow myself to think it could be true. I am so happy right now, being here, and this has been the best moment of my life, having a chance to experience this with you."

As we got up to leave, the same wind hit us both in the face, this time going the other way. We heard the pastor locking up; he'd thought we'd already gone for the night.

Sami and I continued to stay in touch over the years, as he helped me in many ways during my journey in North Africa. Through his faith and belief in his prayers and dreams, he taught me more about faith than anyone ever had before—and that nothing is impossible with God.

Takeaway: Nothing is impossible with God.

THE POST OFFICE

You do not teach the paths of the forest to an old gorilla.

—*Congolese proverb*

Most days, I finished teaching school in the early afternoon, which gave me many opportunities to explore the city and, periodically, the chance to check on my mail at a downtown post office. We did receive mail at the school, but if you had a package sent to you from the States, you had to go into downtown Mombasa to pick it up at the central post office. This was always a crazy experience.

I dreaded going into town because of all the confusion around the post office, with the masses of people coming and going around the center of town. Some days you could see fires burning in trashcans like a war zone.

TAKEAWAYS FROM THE AFRICAN CONTINENT

Going to get my package at the post office that day was unlike any of my previous trips into town. As I rounded the corner from the post office to find a parking space, I was totally surprised to find a spot just outside the building. I was feeling very lucky, as this never happens because most times you always had to park in a shady back lot behind the post office and there was always a chance of getting your car towed or broken into, or even that a beggar might be found taking a nap in the front seat of your car upon your return.

After I parked my car, I started to cross the street but noticed that a young Kenyan boy was standing near the driver's side door. I brushed this off to chance, as many young kids in the city will pour dirty water on your car and then try to wash it off for money. This movement by the boy was what it looked like, until I glanced back from across the street and noticed he had a screwdriver in his hand—he was going to try to break into my car.

I quickly darted back across four lanes of traffic toward my car. I grabbed him just in time, put him in a chicken wing, and started yelling, "Help! I have caught a thief!" I guess, in my mind, this was the right thing to do, but I had forgotten that thieves have a reputation of being the lowest of people in Kenya and bring the most shame to a family. I have seen thieves running in the streets of Mombasa before with burning tires around them and a crowd chasing behind, yelling, "Mwezi!" or thief.

No sooner had I spoken the word "thief," the crowd started gathering around my car. I quickly realized I was about to see mob justice firsthand. I could hear the shop owners slamming their shop doors as the crowd got bigger by the minute, as if a show were about to begin. The crowd started yelling, "Stone him! Stone him!" As I held the thief by the arm, an old lady took off her shoe and started beating the young boy on the head. She asked me if I wanted her to flog him, like he was a personal effect I had caught. I said no, to just get the police.

Before I could find the police, though, the mob grabbed the young boy from my grasp and started to beat him profusely. In the process, I got hit as well and decided I needed to make a run for it and turn him loose to the crowd. As I looked up from the crowd, to my surprise, I saw Patty standing in front of the post office outside the main door. Her eyes caught mine, and she knew I was in trouble; the crowd was heading straight for her. The young boy was crawling across the street on all fours, directly in front of her, bloody and beaten from the mob.

As I tried to wiggle between the masses of people, I felt a hand on my shoulder. It was a Rastafarian-looking guy with dreadlocks and a long beard, which isn't common in Mombasa. He said, "I will take you across the street to the American girl I saw standing on the corner." The only person he could have been talking about was Patty. As he pulled me out of the crowd, the police arrived. But it was too late. As I reached Patty, the young boy collapsed, almost right in front of her, and appeared to be dead. We both made a run for it down a side street, back toward my car, trying to get away from the crowd that had gathered for mob justice.

TAKEAWAYS FROM THE AFRICAN CONTINENT

As we arrived back at the school, the first person I saw was Amos, our headmaster, who asked why I looked so out of sorts. I told him all the details of the ordeal, and he looked puzzled for a moment, then said, "I would have flogged him myself if I had been there." I knew I was no longer in the States when I heard this comment, as many Kenyans have been robbed and want instant revenge in those types of situations.

Takeaway: You can never predict what your guardian angel will look like—possibly even a Rastafarian with dreadlocks.

HEART LANGUAGE

Wisdom is like a baobab tree: No one individual can embrace it.

—*African proverb*

What does it mean to understand a "heart language"? This was the question I asked myself many times during my stay in Africa. It always baffled me when people I was around knew exactly what I was going to do before I said it. As I learned the heart language of a small country in Africa called Derja, I came to realize that heart words meant more than actual words in term of relationships and the narratives you would find yourselves in many days.

This group think idea is strange to us in the West, as our social media does bind us together, but as an individualistic culture, we cannot understand oral cultures and heart languages. Even in our technological advancement in the West, we still miss the opportunities to clearly speak into the situation with specific words of encouragement or just know what exactly to do without having to use words. We want to guess meanings of words based on our own experiences and figure out the context as the situation arises. When you learn a heart language, you understand the meanings words carry with them, which goes beyond their actual, literal meanings. The sounds of the words you hear are very different than the meanings of them when they are used in a heart language situation. I will never forget an example of this heart language idea and how something I read in the Bible came out of my heart and into an invitation letter from a meeting I'd had earlier with some sports people in North Africa.

Many afternoons, I would have a chance to spend some quiet time at my home relaxing or meditating on things I may have read or seen during the week. One afternoon around three o'clock or so, I heard the postman slide a letter under my door. During my quiet time earlier in the week, I had been reading about a man named Felix in the Bible. As I went down to get the letter, I opened this up, and the letter had been addressed to Felix Hix. You cannot imagine how my heart jumped and that the man who addressed this letter was able to understand what I had been reading earlier. This is a heart language example that transcended time and space.

CHRISTOPHER HIX

Takeaway: Tunisians taught me to have a unique understanding of myself and my relationship with words—when their meaning comes from the heart and not the head.

WHITE PLASTIC CHAIRS

Cross the river in a crowd, and the crocodile won't eat you.

—*African proverb*

The day started like any other day in Tunisia by taking the kids to school at the end of the street. After the kids were picked up for school, I noticed as I walked back home that there were some white plastic chairs stacked outside my house beside the garage door. In Tunisia, white plastic chairs have come to signal that either a wedding or death in the family is about to happen. On my way back to my house, my landlord stopped me as I was walking inside my gate to explain what was going on. He told me that his sister had passed away during the night and asked if I would help him with the funeral arrangements since his sons were out of town.

As we went inside his house, we could see that all the neighborhood ladies were in the process of preparing the body. As a flurry of phone calls were made, the neighborhood responded at lightning speed to get everything in place for the burial. After the body was washed and prepared by the women and then wrapped in a white sheet, my landlord and I carried his sister outside from an upstairs room to be placed into a big truck to be taken to the mosque for noon day prayers. As is custom in Muslim culture, the Koran was being played very loudly on a stereo as we carried the body out of a crowded house.

As we got closer to the truck, the crowd gently nudged me toward the inside of the truck. Because I didn't want to drop the body, I put one foot on the bumper. Before I could stop, the crowd pushed me inside the truck with the family—and the body was in between all of us. The truck was cold and sterile, and you could hear the call to prayers in the streets as we drove by each neighborhood. Watching the whole community walking behind the truck was bizarre, not to mention that being American in a situation like this was unheard of.

I learned a valuable lesson during this time that if you live with a family, you are part of that family, regardless of your nationality. Also, the aspects of the death process are so different in North Africa. In the States, we have attempted to make the death process convenient, and it has spun out of control in terms of costs and upgrades related to burials. Why does any family member have to be subjected to five different burial packages in the States, the way they would be if they

TAKEAWAYS FROM THE AFRICAN CONTINENT

were buying a car? We have lost simplicity and have altered the natural lifecycle through embalming and upgrades, from the headstone to the coffin that matches the suit the person is wearing.

They buried my landlord's sister that day for about fifty US dollars, and she was treated with all the respect of a dignitary. I saw family and community come together to help in all areas of this process. They all had a sense that, when it was their time to go, the same respect and honor would be given to them. They are not disconnected from the events and realities of everyday life. This was truly a beautiful thing to see and experience.

Takeaway: If you live with a family, you're part of them—no matter your nationality. Family is family.

DUNCAN, THE HEADMASTER, AND AN ANGEL AT THE GATE

Every door has its own key.

—*Swahili proverb*

My friend Duncan was a slim, funny-looking person from the upcountry of Kenya and part of the majority ethnic group called the Kikuyus. Most Kenyans are mild-tempered, and Duncan was no exception. He always had a smile on his face. I cannot tell you how many times we would sit in his office and he would tell me about how nice it was in the upcountry, in the Rift Valley—"The real Kenya," he always said. He came to the coast of Mombasa for the teaching job, but being surrounded by three hundred mosques and the Islamic culture was draining for him; Duncan was from a Christian family. Working in Mombasa was

TAKEAWAYS FROM THE AFRICAN CONTINENT

hard with a majority Muslim population because he faced persecution daily for his faith.

Late one night, I heard a bang on my gate. It was a small girl who looked to be a student, but I had never seen her before. I guessed she must have known that I was friends with Duncan. She looked very upset. She said Duncan was being held at the police station and was being beaten. I ran to get some clothes on and try to find my keys go to the police station. When I arrived at the station, the time was around midnight, and the police would not let me see Duncan. He was being held behind the counter in a small room. I was surprised that he was being held, as he was the assistant headmaster at the school, and I thought he was respectfully known around town for his role in the community.

I was met at the office by the big officials, but all I wanted to do was see Duncan. Finally, after about an hour, they led me to a back room, where Duncan was sitting. His glasses had been broken, and he was in pain from the electric shock he had received. I asked him what he had been charged for, and he said that he'd left his ID card in his apartment when the police stopped him on the streets as he was walking home. I thought this punishment was over the top, but it was motivated more by ethnic differences and religion than anything else. I had to prove to them that he was employed at the school, but I did not have an identification card to show the police, so the process took a long time. Once Duncan was released, all of his possessions were dumped into a bowl and handed to me, which struck me as kind of funny.

After about two hours, he was finally released, and we were able to go home. I had never really seen someone experiencing persecution because of their faith, but I am sure Duncan did not shy away from sharing his faith while he was being held. I still never found out who the girl was who alerted me about Duncan. I have come to believe that, in Africa, your guardian angels are always working overtime to protect you—in many different forms.

Takeaway: God is faithful to those who are bold in sharing their faith.

A QUIET MILITARY

A family tie is like a tree: it can bend, but it cannot break.

—*African proverb*

M any times, when I was going across the bridge from the school to go home in Mombasa, I noticed a large crowd standing around, and at times, it looked like a riot. One day when this happened, I didn't really know which way to return home. I thought maybe it was because the president was in town for a visit. As I pressed into the crowd, I overheard someone say that something had happened down on the coast toward Somalia and that a hotel had been blown up by a terrorist group. The leader of the group of Kenyans was explaining to the crowd what had happened when an American Apache helicopter suddenly flew overhead; the crowd did not even notice what type of plane it was, which signaled a military presence in the country.

I knew I needed to get back to the school to get more information, but the road was blocked by many people standing in front of the causeway. I had a friend close by who worked at the eye clinic in town, and so I thought I would go to his shop for a while until the crowd abated enough to cross the bridge. The word on the street was that a Jewish-owned hotel had been blown up by extremists down on the coast of Mombasa. I continued to see American military ships and planes coming into Mombasa Harbor, so I decided to look more into the situation when I returned home.

The news came out in the newspaper that an American Apache helicopter had been shot down in Somalia. I really took the news hard because I knew they would take hostages. Soon after, they released photos of the pilots, who had been taken and tortured. The whole situation seemed strange because the US military denied they had a presence in country and they had not been in the harbor with any type of combat ships.

One day in town soon after that event, I happened to run into a young American military captain named Wayne, and we struck up a great conversation. He had some downtime, so I invited him to come to the school where I worked to teach a class on flying helicopters. This time of teaching for Wayne was special because he was able to differentiate the Kenyan school kids from the military conflict he came to Africa to fight. Having personal time with the kids meant the world to him.

TAKEAWAYS FROM THE AFRICAN CONTINENT

Another situation where I observed a quiet military presence happened to me during the Tunisian Revolution in 2011. Almost overnight, the Tunisian military began moving tanks and other heavy equipment out of the desert to address the situation. The tanks looked like camels in a single-file line as they navigated through the sands. The military was the saving grace that prevented a bloodbath in the small country of nine million. The people were so thankful to have the military in all the small towns that the local people would make food for the young men who were very far from home and would stop traffic to give it to them at the roundabouts. The military saved the Tunisian people, and because of their quiet presence, only around three hundred people were killed in the revolution instead of thousands.

Takeaway: Do not always believe what you are being told, especially if what you observe is the opposite.

"WEEKENDS" ON THE COAST OF AFRICA

A united family eats from the same plate.

—Baganda proverb

Saturday mornings usually began with the water carts waking me up early, as the Kenyans went out into the streets around five or so to gather water for the day. The three hundred mosques close to the school all sounded out in unison, as well. The funny thing about my house was that we never consistently had water in the pipes, so you could never turn the water off and on from the faucet. The apartment had a large water tank on top of the house that collected water from the rainstorms and from the pipes when the water was cut on.

Many nights, we would be awakened by the sound of water being pumped on to the roof and the sound of water filling and hitting the

TAKEAWAYS FROM THE AFRICAN CONTINENT

tin container. I would always jump up out of bed as fast as possible to take a shower or wash clothes in the middle of the night. Many times, when the Kenyan politicians would come to town, and depending on whether the zoning of the neighborhood was favorable, we would get water in our pipes. I asked one day where the water came from, and my friend David, who lived behind us, said that some water source came from a river just outside the city where hippos liked to play and bathe in the water. To say the least, I started closing my mouth while in the shower after I heard that important piece of information. I still, to this day, have a hard time taking a shower for longer than three minutes, knowing what a blessing it is to have running water in your pipes all the time.

During my morning routine, the monkeys in the trees outside my house would begin warming up their arms with mangos that they would throw in the yard—and occasionally throw at any innocent passerby. I swear, they kept a small stockpile just for me, for whenever I walked outside of my house. I always got one thrown at me. I would throw it back if it wasn't too rotten, but I never had any luck hitting one of them.

Between the crows and the monkeys, I did not sleep well for two years. Some mornings on my way to the causeway and market, I had this crazy idea that an Egg McMuffin sandwich would be great; that it would be wonderful to have a McDonald's on the corner. No sooner than I'd say this, I would see a guy walking on the bridge straight toward me, wearing a full-blown McDonald's outfit, complete with the hat and shoes. I thought I was seeing things, and if he'd handed me a biscuit, I would have thought he was an angel.

He walked by my car without even looking at me to see if I'd imagined him. The guy behind him had a NASA space shirt on, so I came back to reality. Many African countries get donated clothes from the West, and Kenya is no exception. My favorite shirts were always the bowling and mechanic's shirts with American names on the front pockets. My headmaster loved this clean white shirt that had "The Pantry" written on it. I didn't have the heart to tell him the origin of his favorite work apparel.

Takeaway: Always be thankful for water that is coming out of your pipes or finding a dry shirt with your name on it.

BUNDLING

A patient man will eat ripe fruit.

—*African proverb*

As we traveled back and forth to the States over the years, the idea of bundling had always sounded funny to me. I have always wondered why this concept sounds appealing to us in the States. Why did it seem to cost less if something was bundled together?

During my time in Africa, bundling meant putting a cord around something, either wood or tools, but no doubt it would be carried around on one's shoulders—not through cable or high-speed Internet connections. I even remember the first time someone mentioned what "Internet" meant and how surprised we were to conceptualize this idea. I lived in a small seaside town in North Africa for many years, and we always had a dial-up connection for Internet. This speed seemed to be fine until the capital city started getting high-speed Internet. Then all the small towns outside the capital thought they should have it as well. This was such a strange concept for my neighborhood, which was only sixty miles north of the capital.

I decided one day to enquire about the possibility of getting high-speed service, but I knew it would be a process, as most people where I lived didn't even have very good phone service. I went into the phone company one day to begin to enquire about Internet and was told that they only had a few lines available; I could put my name on a list, and they would call me about setting it up. I walked away, not really thinking about it or how it would work. As we do in Africa, we give something about a year to settle down.

After waiting some time, I went by to check on things, and the sales lady told me to hold on for a minute, that I needed to see a certain person. As I waited, I noticed a small truck outside the store with a huge roll of what seemed like high-speed Internet cable on it. When the man came out of his office, he told me he had some good news: I could have high-speed Internet, but we would have to run the cable from the center of town to my house. I was not that surprised, but that would be a big deal, and I would also have to help him dig the line about a mile or so to my house.

But how important really was it? I guess that was the lesson. About two years later, I received a call that they finally had a way to get me high-speed service. I learned to wait without anticipating anything. I

TAKEAWAYS FROM THE AFRICAN CONTINENT

could usually log on and then go downstairs and make a cup of coffee, go outside and talk to my neighbors, and then go back upstairs to eventually get online. The day I realized that we had high-speed Internet, getting online happened way too fast for me to make a cup of coffee.

Takeaway: Quickly determine how important something is to you and how long you're willing to wait for it, and then you will find the value.

MOUNT KENYA

He who thinks he is leading, and has no one following him, is only taking a walk.

—*African proverb*

During our school breaks from teaching in Mombasa, Patty and I would always try to do something interesting that involved traveling. Preparing for our trip upcountry would take about a week or so, but we were ready to set out on our adventure. On one of our breaks, we contacted a friend in a town called Jill who lived outside of Nairobi and asked if we could stay with her and take off from there to hike Mount Kenya.

Mount Kenya, we were told, was one of the fastest hikes up a mountain in Africa, but going up too fast could cause problems with oxygen. We would need all the help we could get. Even though we were excited about the hike, we had never hiked a serious mountain

TAKEAWAYS FROM THE AFRICAN CONTINENT

before. We drove all day and into the evening and finally arrived in the upcountry. The Rift Valley was blessed with acacia and jacaranda trees and a beautiful, green landscape. The jacaranda trees were in full bloom with their bright purple flowers . . . a much-needed change in scenery from the vegetation on the coast.

When we arrived that night, we set a plan in motion to hike Mount Kenya with three other students from the States who were living in the area. Early the next morning, we drove out close to the base of Mount Kenya, a long, steady incline into the mountains. Our driver knew about a place where we could collect some gear. There would be guides who knew the terrain and could provide us with insight into our journey.

As we approached the village, I knew that our trip was going to be a difficult one, as we were in a tourist trap and the local guides were hungry for money. To begin the hiking trip, we were escorted to a small room behind a store where you could see ski equipment in piles against the door, from boots to coats to poles and other things of that nature. My first thought was, "How did this equipment get in there?" A guide told me that most of the stuff was left by rich Europeans who didn't want to take it back with them, as they needed space for souvenirs.

The equipment looked like a sporting goods store; all of it was in good shape and well-made, in stark contrast to most of the guides, who were wearing flip-flops and old T-shirts and smoking cigarettes. I came to find out later why all the hiking stuff had just been sitting, unused. They asked us to sit down around a pot of boiling chai. It seemed like an elders' meeting of sorts in a sweat lodge.

The room was barely lit, and I quickly realized it was going to be a meeting about what we would be willing to pay to have guides take us up the mountain. Nobody we came with spoke Swahili or a Luo dialect that was spoken around the Mount Kenya area. You could have cut the air with a *panga*, a large knife, as the negotiations started about our trip. One man jumped up and said, "I will take them up the mountain for one thousand Kenyan shillings."

I leaned over to Patty and said, "We are going to get taken advantage of, and the trip could be dangerous."

She punched me in the arm and said, "Relax. It'll all be okay once we start hiking and get into the outdoors and nature."

Our contact agreed to pay them half now and the rest after the trip. The guides were arguing with one another about whether they would get paid if we didn't make it up the mountain. This seemed to be a contentious point, at least by the loud conversation, and it seemed they must have been burned by tourists in the past, or, as we'd seen in the room, they'd been paid in ski gear. It would be hard to feed one's family on used ski equipment.

We told them we would meet them at the base of the mountain in the morning to begin the trip. As we drove away, we could still hear them arguing about the arrangement of the payments. The payment plan would come back to haunt us during the hike as things progressed toward reaching the summit and the weather got worse.

TAKEAWAYS FROM THE AFRICAN CONTINENT

We all woke early the next morning ready for the drive to the base of Mount Kenya, where we met five guides, called porters, who would carry our things so we could hike. The funny thing about the guides: they were wearing flip-flops and smoking cigarettes, as they'd done the day before, and I'd thought they would have been more appropriately dressed for the terrain.

We all piled into a Land Rover and drove for about two hours before coming to a place where the road stopped and the woods began. After hiking halfway to base camp, I was already dizzy from the change in altitude and we were only at the start of our journey. One of the Peace Corps students on the trip had cooked a big bag of soup for us to eat that night. As we began to try to set up camp, I realized that we were having altitude sickness and that we could not locate any utensils with which to eat. We were all laughing about our situation.

We finally managed to eat what was left of the soup, as most of it had spilled out in my backpack, and that was our dinner for the night.

Everyone was exhausted, so we all decided to turn in for bed early. At about three in the morning, I needed to go outside the tent to use the bathroom, but as I looked outside, I saw the largest animal I had ever seen in my life. I thought it was a water buffalo, but what was the animal doing in these woods? It was sniffing the opening to our tent, smelling the soup that had poured out of my backpack. I thought it was coming inside our tent to get some more food. I woke everybody up immediately. You could see this huge silhouette in the shadows of the tent lining, and it looked like a T. rex or something. We were all terrified but laughing loudly. Eventually, the animal went away. What was funny was that there were no guides around, and I don't remember them being close enough at the time to even check in on us.

We packed our things early in the morning and set out for base camp, about ten thousand feet or so up the mountain. It was a beautiful hike until the elevation began to play tricks with our minds. Also, the guides never really slowed down, and I wondered if they had even been paid for the trip, given the way they were acting. We finally landed at the base camp. It had a small site and a lodge for people to sleep in. We did not have much money, so we chose to sleep outside with the hyraxes (a small animal that looks like a big rat) until we could make the ascent to the top of the mountain the next morning.

We tried to set up camp, but most of us had altitude sickness. We wandered around bumping into one another, finding it extremely difficult just to prepare our meal. I walked around the camp and went inside the cabin. I noticed that all guides had a place to sleep and a fire going in the firepit. I didn't really think about it, but the weather could shift at any minute at that altitude. For the moment, it was peaceful, and we were getting excited to get a chance to reach the summit of a mountaintop the next day.

We turned in for the night, but at about four or so in the morning, a Kenyan with a flashlight on his cap woke all of us by shaking off the snow that had fallen on our tent overnight. The weight of the snow had partially collapsed our tent. After we all dressed and went outside, the Kenyan guides were standing around with full ski gear on, snow

TAKEAWAYS FROM THE AFRICAN CONTINENT

boots, gloves, goggles and flashlights on their heads. Just a day before, all the guides were wearing flip-flops and T-shirts! They were yelling for us to get ready to go before all the snow set in.

I could not see a thing outside the tent, as we were in a whiteout situation. I was becoming nervous because we only had on tennis shoes and the minimal snow gear, and they were expecting us to ascend a mountain where we would be going over sharp rocks and loose stones in the snow. I had a bad feeling that someone might slip and fall and die on the mountain. I had to make a quick decision, as everybody was out of it. I went outside the tent and told the guides we needed to wait and stay put for a while.

After the snow stopped, I could hardly get out of the tent. It had piled up to about five inches or so. I decided for the group that it would be best for us to return down the mountain and try to make it to the top another time. I was at peace with this, but Patty was livid, to say the least. She complained the whole way back down the mountain about how we would always regret that decision. When we finally made it back down to the original base camp, we ran into a group that was going up the mountain, so a Land Rover that had dropped them off was available.

The trip really began to take a turn for the worst as we all got into the car. It was pouring down rain, and the mud was very slippery. One British man was in the back of the van in distress. All he could say was "I want to go home." As the van started down the hill, it began to slip and slide, hanging over the side of the mountain every time we would take a turn. The driver almost went over the embankment more times than I could count. It was as though he were trying to kill us all. I have never said so many prayers in my life. I held on to Patty as tightly as I ever had before.

Once we made it back down the hill, tempers flared. They thought that because we didn't go to the top of the summit, we weren't going to pay them for the entire trip. The ride that was going to pick us up, and who had negotiated the trip, was running late, and we were being held in a small room waiting for him to arrive. I'm not sure what would have happened to us if he hadn't shown up that day. Two hours later, he finally came, and as he walked up to the store, a Kenyan pulled out a gun and demanded payment for his guides. I told Patty to look in my pack and find any money that I had and give it to them. She hurried and found a wad of shillings and handed it to them as we jumped into the car and sped off down the winding dirt road and headed back to our home, exhausted from the whole encounter.

Takeaway: When your hiking guides go from smoking cigarettes and wearing flip-flops to putting on oxygen masks and Gore-Tex clothing, you need to rethink your chances of reaching the summit in tennis shoes— your life is in danger.

ALL-NIGHT WEDDINGS IN NORTH AFRICA

Marriage is like a groundnut: You have to crack it to see what is inside.

—*African proverb*

Weddings in North Africa are one of the most significant occasions in the community. I went to a wedding one time that lasted about seven days and included feeding all the neighbors and surrounding villages. During the wedding, the bride is picked up and brought to the ceremony on a camel in a type of carriage fixed atop of the animal. This was an incredible connection for them, going back to their historical roots in North Africa. I came to understand the Berbers' connection to the camel and what it represents for many people, especially the nomadic peoples of southern Tunisia.

Once the bride climbs atop the camel, the door to the carriage is closed. It's really hot inside, especially in the summer. The bride has her own entourage of family and friends that walk alongside her through the streets of her hometown all the way to the groom's house. There, the party and the long process of putting everything together begin. When the bride arrives at the groom's house, everything has been prepared beforehand, from pots and pans in the kitchen to bedrooms complete with beds and sheets, really everything in the house; it's all in place.

When the whole processional comes to an end, the groom takes the key and opens the house for the bride to come inside. Then a traditional band begins to play, and there is incense burning throughout the house in celebration. The community is fed every day for a solid week or more by the bride's family, and they always host with colorful decorations, music, and dancing.

This is a time of family and community on a level that is hard to compare to anything I've experienced in the US.

Takeaway: Always be ready to be carried away by a camel, and make sure you have the key to your house with you or you will sleep outside for a lifetime.

ONE-FORK WEDDING CAKE

He who loves the vase, loves also what is inside.

—*African proverb*

The high school team I was teaching with in Mombasa was made up of young, educated, and bright teachers from all over Kenya, and many were from different tribes as well. The Kenyans spoke a common language of Swahili, but each teacher also had a heart language. Because many of the teachers were single, we were always getting invitations to weddings. Weddings in Africa can last upward of two weeks sometimes. Due to the British colonization of Kenya, many of the weddings took on elements of Western culture, which usually meant that an educated teacher would try to take only two or three days for the ceremony.

My friend, the science teacher Mr. Matui told me one day at the school that he was planning to get married. Mr. Matui was tall and slender, and a member of the Luo Tribe in Kenya. He used to wear this pink shirt with a kitten on it for some reason. He never thought about the color. Patty and I decided that we would attend the wedding all day on Saturday.

When we arrived, we were seated in an open-air tent with chairs underneath the big top. There were about a thousand people sitting under it, with the couple on a stage sitting side by side. As I looked up, I noticed that they had put two more chairs beside the couple for us to sit in for the ceremony. I whispered under my breath to Patty that we were the special guests.

Walking up the aisle felt like I was getting married myself, and after we sat, I noticed that the bride and groom had unhappy looks on their faces. I came to understand later that Kenyans were required to project this look on their faces to signal to their families that they really wanted to stay with them. So, after about five hours of many wedding rituals, from jumping over brooms to signing documents, they finally brought out a huge cake that had been sitting out in the open and was now leaning slightly to the left. The room was still full of guests who were waiting for something to eat, so they began to serve the cake at the back of the tent, one by one—and they only had one fork for everyone to use to eat the cake.

Because we were the guests of honor seated up front with the bride and groom, we realized we would be served last. After what seemed

TAKEAWAYS FROM THE AFRICAN CONTINENT

like an eternity, waiting for all the guests to eat the cake with just one fork, it was now our time. I really didn't want to eat the last bite of cake using this shared fork, but I had no choice. I tried to just use my teeth to slide the piece of cake off the fork, but the person feeding me turned up the fork like they were feeding a baby, so I had to bear it and bite down on the fork. I kept the cake down, but it was even harder for Patty. We always laugh at this story and wonder how we made it through that experience.

Takeaway: For any event you've been invited to in Africa, carry a plastic fork with you or be prepared to eat with your hands.

REVOLUTIONS AND YOUTUBE VIDEOS

An army of sheep led by a lion can defeat an army of lions led by a sheep.

—*Ghanaian proverb*

The following story occurred right after the revolution happened on Saturday afternoon, when the president had left the country in search of asylum. The whole day was surreal. The moment he left the country, our Internet went from dial-up speed to high speed in seconds. The reason this was so funny was that for twenty-three years as technology developed, Tunisia had had only one server through which the Internet flowed. Internet was controlled by the government, and you had only very restricted sites which you could view. When the whole country went online after the revolution, you could hear families laughing in their houses from YouTube videos, as they were now able to search the Internet for information or entertainment and enjoy it like the

TAKEAWAYS FROM THE AFRICAN CONTINENT

rest of the world. The Internet controls had been lifted, and the Internet had become an open source of information.

I'll never forget the first YouTube video we watched as a family. It was about a German submarine captain who was just beginning to learn the English language. As the frantic voice on the other end of the radio was shouting "Mayday, we are sinking. . . . We are sinking," the captain reluctantly responded, "What are you sinking about?" We watched this video at least fifty or so times and laughed so hard we could be heard out in the street by our language tutor.

As I walked through my neighborhood, I could hear other families laughing as well and having fun with the new opportunity to surf the web. Our neighborhood became more communal than ever before, and many of the gates to houses remained unlocked at that time. Children were pitching in to help with neighborhood services that were no longer available like sidewalk sweeping, trash collection, and securing barricades on the corners to protect their streets.

To be in another country when it's liberated as an American citizen, surrounded by nine million other oppressed people suddenly free, is something I will never forget. I didn't realize that I had become oppressed myself like the Tunisians I had lived among and I had absorbed the fearful lifestyle of one controlled by a dictator. I felt wonderful and free to be a part of something that had been long overdue. I'm sure this experience will probably never happen to me again in my lifetime.

I remember riding with some of my Tunisian friends in a car shortly after the revolution, and we got behind a truck carrying donkeys. They said in Arabic, "That is how we have been living for the last twenty-three years. We have been carried around in the back of a truck, with no ability to see what was ahead and no hope for the future."

Takeaway: All people want to have freedom, to raise their families in peace, and to strive for a life that allows hope for the future.

HOLY WATER AND AIRPORT SCANNERS

There are many colorful flowers on the path of life, but the prettiest have the sharpest thorns.

—*African proverb*

During my time overseas, I traveled many times into the Middle East. At certain times of the year on the flights back to North Africa, I would encounter many people who had made a spiritual pilgrimage to the Middle East and were now returning home. Although I never made the pilgrimage myself, I did enjoy the cheap flights during the season. Many people were coming back from Saudi Arabia from the holy month of Ramadan. They would all be dressed in white clothing, and they would always be carrying holy water in these silver containers they would put under the seats. These containers made it very difficult to relax or stretch out, not to mention when one of them would fall over and spill.

On one trip when I was returning to Tunisia, I realized that many of the people were Berbers from Algeria. This made it special for me, as I had many friends who were Berbers. The only problem was that most people on the plane had never flown before, and they were all nervous about what to do when it came time to disembark to catch another plane. The one thing that was clear was that all of the people had containers of holy water from Mecca, and that was going to be a huge problem getting them through the airport scanners. I felt like if I didn't take some sort of action, I may never make it home myself. So, I made my way to the front of the line and began to speak to the young guard who was checking baggage. I asked if we could maybe pass the containers of holy water around the outside of the scanners so folks wouldn't beep every time one of the containers went through the scanner. I was also able to convince the young man that since these guys were all going to the same place, just to let the people hold the containers in their laps instead of putting them under the plane. Many of the people were elderly, and of course, respect was given to them in ways unlike we would give our seniors in the States in a similar situation.

Takeaway: When you have holy water in containers, always make sure the lid is on tight.

VICTORIA FALLS, ZIMBABWE

Three things cause sorrow to flee: water, green trees, and a beautiful face.

—*Moroccan proverb*

Patty and I loved to travel, and we thought since we were going to North Africa anyway, why not visit another African country we had never been to before. We also wanted to see Victoria Falls, so we chose to camp and do some whitewater rafting in Zimbabwe and Zambia. We both had always wanted to go to Zimbabwe but had just never had the chance or the means to make it happen. I had a contact from a family friend who had a brother who lived in Harare named Bob. I contacted Bob to tell him that I might be coming his way and I wanted to see if he would be around. He wrote back and said he would be there but requested that I bring him some motorboat parts for a fishing boat he'd gotten from the States.

Patty and I landed in Zimbabwe late in the afternoon. The setting sun was so hot and seemed like it was the size of the world. I was glad to see Bob at the ticket counter waiting for us. My friend was an interesting kind of guy. He was a traditional worker from the Bible Belt of South Carolina. His nickname was "One Way" because he had a big finger pointing to the sky on the side of his car. As we drove toward his house, I learned why.

Every time we would see people walking on the street, he would let a flyer go out of the window. Once it hit the ground, you could see all the school kids fighting over it in small piles as we drove by. He had the salvation plan printed on these small leaflets.

When we arrived at his house, he had a large stuffed emu over the entrance to the door, along with many other stuffed animals decorating all the walls of his house. We knew this was going to be a crazy time, but it felt good to be back in Africa again, and it felt like coming home. According to tradition, once you drink the water in Africa, you will always return.

We settled into our room and then had a great dinner with Bob and his wife. We discussed our plans and what we wanted to do during our stay. We decided that we wanted to visit Victoria Falls, one of the seventh wonders of the world. As I told Bob about my plans, he told me about a bus that ran from Harare to Bulawayo, where we could camp, visit the falls, and eventually go whitewater rafting.

Patty and I started out on an adventure once again. I went to the bus station and bought us two tickets to Victoria Falls on what

TAKEAWAYS FROM THE AFRICAN CONTINENT

seemed to be a nice bus. We packed our things, said goodbye to Bob, and started out on our journey. About an hour into the trip, we were stopped by a policeman who wanted to see the bus driver's information, like registration and inspections.

After about an hour or so, the bus company told us that the bus had been shut down and the driver had been taken to jail. It turned out that the driver was possibly an escaped convict who had decided to drive the bus up to the falls. You never know what you're going to find in Africa.

Now we had a decision to make about how we were going to get to Victoria Falls. Patty looked at me and suggested that maybe there was a train in the next town over. We decided to hitchhike and then take local transport to the nearest train station. I went to the ticket office and bought the last two tickets for sale, and they were for the last section of the train next door to the crated animals.

When I turned around, I ran into a South African couple who were planning on going up to the falls as well. They said we could catch a ride with them in first class after we boarded the train. As the train approached the station, it was a beautiful coal/steam engine train still running from the colonial days of British occupation in Zimbabwe. As we jumped onboard, my friend Andy from South Africa told us to go to his room and wait; when the train conductor came by, he would give him our tickets. Patty and I were exhausted by that point, so we agreed that was a good idea.

When the conductor came by, he only punched Andy's tickets, and when the door shut, we took a sigh of relief. After the dust settled, we realized that right beside him, there was an empty room. We jumped into the next room for the all-night ride up to the falls. The inside of the cabin was absolutely beautiful, with mahogany wood closets from floor to ceiling. Patty jumped onto a small pull-out bed that pulled down from the ceiling, and we were on our way. The conductor never came back to check on us, so we rested well and enjoyed watching the beautiful African sunrise from our train window. It was truly amazing. We both realized why we loved Africa so much.

We had arrived at Victoria Falls, and it was truly breathtaking. We said our goodbyes to Andy. I needed to find a place for us to stay that was cheap and close to the falls. One guy I asked said there was a campground with basic conditions, but at least it was a roof over our heads and would be cheap.

We entered through the door, and we both collapsed on the cots—but mine went through and hit the ground. I started laughing and could not get back up off the floor. We found a dive to eat local, cheap food and then went back to a crowded campsite to try to sleep. The campground had a crazy mixture of bohemian people sitting around campfires and European families on a holiday, playing cards at tables in a dim light.

I told Patty that we should try to get some sleep, but the music was too loud and the mattresses were filled with bedbugs. I decided to maybe just lean up against the wall to get some sleep, but Patty fell fast asleep, seeming to have adjusted well, bedbugs and all. As I watched her sleep, I knew that she was my soul mate and would be willing to go with me to all these crazy places while making the experience seem normal. Patty had a gift of making all the crazy places seem like home. That was what I loved about her, along with the many things that she would bring to our relationship. Even in the sweltering heat of Zimbabwe, she looked beautiful, and I was glad that at least one of us was getting some sleep.

My mind raced, thinking about how we would put together a trip the next day to go whitewater rafting in the "Mighty Zambezi," as the locals called it. I finally nodded off when the power went out and the radio next to our tent went off for about an hour. The only problem with having no power was the issue of mosquitoes. They were brutal, and we had not thought about getting a net to cover our beds.

I woke up to the sound of running water, and I could not determine where it was coming from. I poked my head out of my tent and saw a person taking a shower using a pot of hot water that he had to have been heating up over a fire and then pouring over his head to rinse out the soap. This scene took me back to Kenya, when Patty and I had traveled outside of Nairobi to visit some friends thirty miles off a paved road into a rural village. The place our friend had us stay at was a World Health Organization clinic, where all the beds had stirrups attached to them for women giving birth. The memory that stuck the most in my mind was having woken up to a large group of Kenyan kids watching us sleep through the broken glass at the tops of the doors. When I went outside, a Kenyan mama was heating up water for me to take a shower. The flashback to Kenya stopped quickly as hot water hit my tent from a gentleman throwing out his water, which ran into my tent under the door and woke Patty up, as well. Good old Africa and the simplicity of life on that continent.

Since we were up, we decided to go out to look for some breakfast. As we were walking around the campsite, I noticed people getting ready to go rafting, who had all their gear piled up beside a van. I asked about the trip, and the guide told me where to go to sign up for it. We both hurried along until I found the shop that booked the tours. The guy behind the desk said a group was just in the process of going and asked if we would like to join the expedition. I responded yes quickly and asked if they would wait while we grabbed a few things and locked up the tent. We were about to navigate the river with a group of people from South Africa, which was going to be quite an experience. We boarded a small minivan and took off for the falls with helmets and gear in hand.

Takeaway: When you hitchhike on a train, always look for friends who are from South Africa—they will know the way home.

CRITICAL PATH: PAYING FOR NO WATER

Two ants do not fail to pull one grasshopper.

—*Tanzanian proverb*

After living overseas in Africa for many years, one thing you realize is that they find the critical path and cut to the chase about many things. Many nights, I would lock my car up outside my house so the tires wouldn't be stolen. One morning, I came outside to realize that my car was missing two tires and that the tires had been taken with such precision that I had not even heard a sound.

As I went to the market later that day, I noticed a cart that was coming my way. The tires that were on the cart really looked like the ones I'd had on my car. My first instinct was to get mad, and then I realized that they had only taken two tires because that was all that the cart required. I learned a real lesson that morning about only using what you need, even if that meant my tires. I guessed that when the two tires went bad, they would return for the other tires whenever they needed them.

I asked my Kenyan friend David what he thought about the situation, and he said that I would get "used." He was trying to relay that I would get used to it. Over the years, that statement would continue to visit me in many situations because, like the old saying goes, there's a difference between a tire that has a puncture in it and a tire that has no tread.

Many times, I would stand in line to pay my water or phone bill. Most of the month, I didn't have water or electricity in my house, yet I always received a bill. It was as though they took a bill from someone who had lived in the house years before my arrival. As I stood in line, I would visit with people and get caught up asking about their families or children. One time, I made the mistake of asking someone why we were standing in line to pay for a service that we did not receive. He simply said, "We pay the bill in case it comes." I didn't quite know what to make of this, but I went with it and realized it was more about the relationships there in the line and less about paying the bill. I was focused on the service, not who was standing in line with me. *Could I live one day at a time?* I thought.

Finding the critical path is very important in establishing a place where serenity can reside. In African culture, many things that are not important are thrown aside for things that bring a sense of well-being

TAKEAWAYS FROM THE AFRICAN CONTINENT

and simplicity. Family is first, and achievement is filtered through the elders of the family, never forgetting to give them respect and a place to grow old in peace.

Takeaway: Finding the critical path is very important in establishing a place where serenity can reside and live.

THE EVIL EYE

What you give, you get ten times over.

—*Yoruba proverb*

In Africa, this concept of giving back was always very interesting to me, having come from a capitalistic culture where we've been taught to always consume and never replace anything. I cannot tell you how many times my neighbor would out-give someone, depending on what they'd given him. I learned very early on from my experience that if you visited a home, never mention that you liked something in their house. I made the mistake of saying how nice a goat looked one time, and before I could get my things to leave, they had already prepared the goat to leave with me.

The lesson here is to be ready to give something back in place of what you just took or received. It's almost a kind of karma/synergy

TAKEAWAYS FROM THE AFRICAN CONTINENT

thing that will affect your whole day and your relationships. This idea will stay embedded in the daily encounters you have all day long. If you are given a plate of food, you will never return the plate empty. If you give someone something, they will always return the favor with fruit or dates or something but never leave the gesture empty.

Takeaway: Never return an empty plate or take something from someone without doing or giving something thoughtful in return.

WOODEN DENTURES

Beauty is not sold or eaten.

—*Nigerian proverb*

Finding different types of doctors in Africa can be an interesting adventure, as you have to speak in a different language many times and just trust the process. I learned that what seems normal in one culture is not what it appears or what happens in different cultures. Something happens to rational decision-making between cultures when formative experiences clash in interpreting meanings.

One time, Patty and I needed to see a dentist to have our teeth cleaned and address some issues of pain I was having with a cavity. Our adventure began when I decided to have my teeth cleaned and some x-rays taken the week before Patty had scheduled her dentist visit. When I went in to visit the dentist, I had not realized that he would want us to bite down on wooden blocks so he could determine our bite. He had many of these blocks on a shelf in his office. I thought maybe it was just a joke and dismissed this as maybe a fluke. I decided to go ahead with the cleaning first just in case this may not turn out to be a positive experience.

The dentist began to clean my teeth, and he decided that everything looked good, except that I had a cavity that needed to be filled at some point. He made a note of it on his chart. The dentist cleaned my teeth, and he told me that he would fill the cavity the next day because he ran out of time and needed to see other patients. I decided to wait until the next week to fill the cavity, but Patty needed to have her teeth cleaned and decided to use my appointment instead. We thought, surely, there would be no problem with the change of appointments.

Patty and I both went into the dentist's office, talked to them, and made the decision that she would have her teeth cleaned and I would come back the next week to complete my procedure. Patty went in for her appointment, and I was in the waiting room. After the dentist had been cleaning Patty's teeth for about an hour, he called me into the office. He told me her teeth seemed very dirty to have just had them cleaned the day before.

I didn't have a chance to talk to Patty at that point, as she was still in the office chair. I went back out into the lobby and sat down with the sinking feeling that something weird had just happened, that a big mix-up may have occurred. Maybe the dentist thought Patty was me and maybe he just filled a cavity in Patty's mouth—not mine. I thought there was no way that he could have confused Patty with me and then filled a cavity that she obviously didn't have. I sat in the lobby for another thirty minutes, and then the receptionist called me to the window and asked for payment for a filling done on Patty. I did not know what to say.

I went inside the office to see what was happening, and Patty had this crazy look on her face. She motioned for me to say something to the dentist. I asked the dentist what they had done to Patty. The dentist told me that they had given Patty a filling. I could not believe the mix-up. I told the dentist that he had made a mistake, and he acted like nothing happened. The funny thing, too, was that he never apologized and wanted payment for the work on Patty's teeth that he had planned for mine.

On our ride home, Patty told me that she had not really understood what was going on during her procedure and that she could not ask the dentist any questions with her mouth pried open, but she knew that the dentist had been doing more than just cleaning her teeth during the procedure. I told her that at least now she would never have a problem with that tooth ever again.

Takeaway: Always double-check to make sure that the wooden mold the doctor is showing you is the mold of your own teeth and not someone else's.

SEWER DUCKS

However little food we have, we'll share it, even if it's only one locust.

—Malagasy proverb

There is an African proverb that says you should always offer your friend whatever you have. I came to understand this proverb during my time in Africa. Many times, on the weekends, I would visit homes of students who lived close enough to the school and I could walk there. If you were invited into homes, even if they had very little food, they would offer you more than they had. If you walked in on people eating, they would make you sit down and eat with them. You would always be the guest and treated like a king.

One weekend during a break, I went home with a student to eat at his house for dinner. My friend lived in a high-rise apartment that was located close to the center of town. As I entered the building, the first thing I noticed was that there were many small ducklings jumping and playing in the sewer water in front of his house. It was not uncommon to see chickens running around, but baby ducks looked funny. They were bumping off my leg as I stepped over them.

I didn't give the ducks another thought as I climbed the stairs to visit my friends. I knocked on the door and went in and visited with him for a while. Around dinnertime, he told me he had a surprise for me. He prepared dinner and brought it out to the table. He took the lid of off a huge pot and exclaimed, "My friend, we have roasted duck for dinner!" I remembered the ducks I had seen earlier in the street playing in the sewer water.

My friend wanted me to have the best thing he had, and that was his ducks. In African cultures, you eat what's put in front of you. I began to bite down on the duck and realized it had not been cooked long enough for the meat to be soft. It was incredibly chewy and tough. It felt like it took two hours just to chew the meal.

The company of friends was priceless, though, and I realized that not all things were bad and that he would offer me anything he had, even though that might be as small as a duck from the sewer. As I walked back home, I never again looked at street animals in the same way.

Takeaway: Never take for granted where your next meal will come from— or where it might be located.

COFFEE AND LOVE

Coffee and love taste best when hot.

—*Ethiopian proverb*

There's something about Africa that brings coffee and love together; I cannot tell you how many times I found that to be true. It is said that once you taste the water of Africa, you'll always return, and that was true of my experience. After spending thirteen years on the African continent, enjoying love with my family and drinking more cups of coffee than I want to mention were priceless to me.

The coffee in Tunisia is called a "direct" and would put Starbucks to shame, both in price and taste. The nights in Tunisia were filled with love and coffee, from every street corner to every small barista in town. The hustle and bustle of the noise of life was so alive with joy and suffering and the up and downs of living. Living in the Mediterranean climate, you come to appreciate loud conversation, whether peaceful or angry.

The energy around the coffee shops was a combination of an American athletic event and Sunday afternoons, with men from the local community just spending time together playing cards or watching TV. The most important events of the world would unfold on tired, old, black-and-white televisions attached to a hole in the wall, with everyone staring at it. The passion and love of the gathering was a beautiful thing to see. The farmers, the students, the businessmen were always gathered around the table, drinking coffee together, while the women were at home making couscous and talking about the family as they waited for them to return home.

Takeaway: You should never be alone drinking coffee and not feeling the love of your family.

DO YOU HAVE THE OWNER'S MANUAL?

A single bracelet does not jingle.

—*Congolese proverb*

Most of my time in Africa was spent in lines paying for something that usually hadn't happened or for services that had taken sometimes upward of two years to happen. One story that really stands out to me involves my encounter with a washing machine mechanic who wanted to fix my machine that was at the school where I taught. We had a washing machine that had been left by a British family and honestly did not work very well. Because we grew up using machines to wash clothes and not by hand, we thought we would try to use the machine from time to time.

When the machine finally broke, I decided to call somebody. The young man arrived early at my house with all the tools needed to do the job. I showed him the machine and told him I had to go to class and would be back after lunch. When I returned to the house, he had taken the machine apart, piece by piece, and had it laid out perfectly on the floor. I had never seen anything like it before and never realized that a washing machine had so many parts connected to it. I scratched my head a bit before I worked up the courage to ask him what he thought could be wrong with the machine.

As we looked at each other, he said in a beautiful British-Kenyan accent, "Bwana, do you have the owner's manual for the washing machine?" I took a long sigh before answering no. Then I realized that he had just taken the whole machine apart and was asking for the diagram so he could put it back together. He said that he needed the manual to make the decision about what was wrong. I realized that I may have had the only actual washing machine that anyone had ever seen on the coast of Africa.

This experience made me realize that sometimes we have to take a chance on people to figure something out, especially if they have never seen anything like it before. I wanted to get upset but at the same time got a huge laugh out of the time I had spent with the young man.

I have seen a similar pattern happen before in my own life. Just recently, I took a job where the person hiring me thought I had more experience doing what they were asking me to do. It didn't dawn on

TAKEAWAYS FROM THE AFRICAN CONTINENT

them right away that what they wanted me to do wasn't what was happening. In my job performance, I basically said, "Do you have an owner's manual so I can figure this out?"

Takeaway: In life, you have to trust people who do not have an owner's manual to fix something

FOUR-SEASONS LEMON TREE AND WISDOM FROM DJERBA

When you follow in the path of your father, you learn to walk like him.

—*African proverb*

Many times, I would travel to a small island called Djerba, which is off the coast of Africa, close to Libya. It is the most interesting place I've ever visited. The culture is rich with history and religion and is a wonderful clash of Berber, Jewish, and Arab living. One thing I always found interesting was a type of tree on the island called a "four-season lemon tree." It is very unusual in that within its DNA, there are four developmental stages that take place on their branches. You can see all developmental stages, from budding to small fruit to mature fruit.

TAKEAWAYS FROM THE AFRICAN CONTINENT

The plant has always helped me focus on life and the stages we go through. To see the whole life span take place on one branch was very enlightening. If the tree's fruit is not mature enough, it will drop its fruit for the whole plant to survive. We can learn so much about life from this tree—how we can simplify things that really don't matter for our survival. I have always been interested in transitions, and the four-seasons lemon tree reminds me of the many transitions Djerba has been through over several thousand years or so.

The architecture in the city is very interesting and reflects the influence of past invasions. All the houses on the island have windows that are disproportionate to the size of the house, located at the upper half of the house. I asked about it one time during my stay and was told that because the town had been invaded so many times over the centuries, the homeowners built windows higher than a person sitting on a horse. Through the windows was how they broke into houses to steal things, so the people built windows that a person couldn't crawl into from a horse.

Takeaway: Learn how to simplify things in your life so that when transitions come, you will not be weighed down.

GREEN MAMBAS, MONITOR LIZARDS, AND MONKEYS IN YOUR CAR

You learn how to cut down trees by cutting them down.

—African proverb

The country of Kenya had so many different types of animals that always invaded your space, which made for many humorous experiences. We lived on an island called Mombasa, which is on the coast, and the school where I taught was located on the outskirts of the city. The school was located in a rural area with a city-like environment. With it came many different exotic animals.

A man named David who helped me with my yard told me that snakes could be a problem, as well as mosquitoes. Because malaria was such a problem, every month we would wax the floors of the apartment with a type of wax that repelled animals and mosquitoes.

TAKEAWAYS FROM THE AFRICAN CONTINENT

I also noticed that our front door had a two-inch cut up from the ground, where a small animal could crawl under if they wanted to.

One time during dinner, I was standing in the kitchen doorway when I noticed a bright-green snake called a mamba heading straight toward me. Because David and I had just waxed the floors, this snake was moving in an awkward motion, which gave me time to get out of the way a bit. The green mamba is one of the most poisonous snakes in Africa. The snake went between my legs and then behind a closet drawer. I yelled for David, who ran and got a panga, which is a big knife, and cut the thing in half. My heart did not slow down for the whole night.

There was another thing that would always occur on my way to the market, and it never ceased to amaze me. Every time, close to my house, there was a twelve-foot monitor lizard, almost the size of my car, that would come out and cross the road from out of nowhere. I would pull up to him, and he would turn his head and scatter off into the woods. It was bizarre, and I often thought about where he might live in this city.

On the weekends, we had time to take in safaris and visit game parks that were close to us in Mombasa. We were told you should never leave your windows open because monkeys could get into your car and they were very aggressive and could bite. We had monkeys in the trees at our house at the school. Our helper was Kenyan, and what always took me by surprise was that every time David came into the yard, the monkeys would take off, almost as if he had a common practice of throwing something at them. When I would come out of my house to go teach, the monkeys would throw old, half-eaten mangos at me and make a loud, laughing noise. I had some insight and always tried to keep the windows closed when we went to the game parks.

On one occasion, I'd forgotten to roll up the windows, and when we returned to our car, the nightmare I had envisioned had happened. The inside of my car looked like twenty black balls jumping around from window to window. On the hood of the car, there were two monkeys that had twisted my windshield wipers and were drinking the Cokes I'd left in the car and eating potato chips. We sat down, just watched them, and had a good laugh. I wished David had been traveling with me so they would have been scared and run off and I could return home. David told me one day that the monkeys can see color, and they can differentiate between white and black. David said many Kenyans like to eat monkeys, and this is why they run from them. White people, on the other hand, seem to always have treats for them and are afraid of them. Eventually, the monkeys left, but they knew that they had conquered my car. I'd lost the fight, had given in, and enjoyed getting used to it, as David would always tell me to do.

Takeaway: Always remember that animals can see in color and that the color of your skin may be what scares them off or attracts them.

SOLITUDE FROM THE DESERT AND A BERBER STATE OF MIND

Knowledge without wisdom is like water in the sand.

—African proverb

While I was in North Africa, I traveled into the desert and was always taken back by the vastness of the landscape and the quietness of the place. The people I traveled with would tell stories of many different things during our time in the desert. What struck me as being different was that they would always have two camels traveling together. I asked one time what the logic was behind taking two camels, and they told me this truth: In the desert, it is very hard to find water, so they have one camel fill up on water to the point that it cannot drink any more. Over the long trip in the desert, the caravan would use the extra camel for food. During the process of cleaning the animal, they would boil the water they retrieved from the stomach of the camel.

There's another story that I could hardly believe until they told me how they found water in the desert. They would try to locate a small animal called a dik-dik. This little animal looks like a small gazelle, jumps back and forth and up and down, and is very active and high-strung. As the story goes, this animal can smell water even in the remotest part of the landscape. The Berbers begin to look for this desert friend at any point during their trip. What a joy it must be when nomadic peoples locate this small animal. It's very interesting to think that water can be smelled in the air, but with the right kind of nose, you can be led to this discovery. They trust this small messenger to bring them life, give information, and find a possible location for water.

The houses that the Berbers lived in were called *ksours*. These were fortified structures usually set atop a large mountain-type structure and could be defended from the Arab invasions. These houses were family friendly, and each room was located off a central open space, which acted as an air conditioner in the summer time.

I was amazed at the simple way of life these precious groups lived. They took one day at a time, and they had a flow about them that was always within the structure of the relationship brought about by the emphasis on family. I was fortunate to call them my friends and had a chance to learn their ways and customs, which changed my life forever.

One story I'll never forget is the time we visited a small town in southern Tunisia where John Lucas had filmed the bar scene in *Star Wars*. I was visiting a small shop owner in the town, who I'd known from past visits. After I bought a few things from his shop, I decided to give him an audio tape, which was a recording in a Berber dialect about stories from the Bible. After I left his shop, my friends and I decided to ride around and check out other things in the town, then continue on to the coast to the island of Djerba.

As we left the town, I noticed that all roads were being blocked and each car was getting stopped by police at a checkpoint. This wasn't really uncommon, as that part of the country was very controlled. We pulled up to the checkpoint and saw that a young police officer had the tape I'd given the shop owner in his hand. My heart sank, as I knew what he was going to ask us. I was traveling with four other Americans in a very small car. The officer asked for identification and started asking questions about the tape.

My initial reaction was to act like I had no idea what he was talking about and he would have possibly moved us along. We all gave him our passports, and I had my visa but had mistakenly brought my wife's instead of mine, which did not help the situation. I eventually got out of the car and began to talk to the young officer. After about an hour or so, the officer decided that we would be taken into the

National Guard office to be questioned. They wanted to figure out what was going on.

We turned the car around and headed back into town, where they took us into the compound, put my friends in the back, and then began to question me about the tape. This experience went on for many hours until one of the friends I was traveling with became very nervous and upset, soiled his pants, and needed to get a change of clothes. What this action meant was that he needed to get in the trunk of the car to get a change of clothes. I was concerned that there may have been more tapes in plain sight that would have taken our situation to a deeper level, as certain material was considered solicitation and was illegal to give out in the country.

We went to my car and opened the trunk. I wasn't sure which piece of luggage belonged to my friend. I was able to get him some new clothes to put on, and the police officers had not seen anything in the truck that had made them suspicious. We all went back into the station, and the questioning continued all day and into the night. As they listened to the tape, they had so many questions about it, about the meaning behind it. Around ten or so that night, another person in our group started violently throwing up, having become very sick. I don't know why, but that particular thing really affected them, and they had compassion for us.

Around midnight, they finally released us from this situation. One of the funniest things that happened at that point was as we were driving out of town, an off-duty police officer asked us if we had more of these tapes he could give to his family. I almost said, "Hey, just wait a minute. I have more"—and then my friend punched me in the arm and said, "We're good." We all had the biggest laugh you can imagine, and the experience bonded us together for life.

Takeaway: Never underestimate the ability or the ways that bodily fluids can be used to get you out of certain situations.

RUNNING A MARATHON BAREFOOT IN A PINK CAMISOLE—AND CAN YOU SEE ME, MAMA?

To run is not necessarily to arrive.

—*Swahili proverb*

This story makes me laugh to this day when I think about it. At our home in Kenya, we lived on a compound that was contained within the school property. Outside of the main house was a small, one-room house where a young man named David lived who would help with yard work and other things around the house. We had many people who came from the States to volunteer as teachers at the school over the years. Usually, after the two-year assignment was over, many different articles of clothing and goods had to be left at the school or put in the back room at the house. I would visit with David from time to time and would notice all this stuff he had piled up in the corner of his room.

One afternoon when I'd finished teaching, I returned to the house to take a rest and noticed outside our window, hanging on the clothesline, was a pink camisole that looked like it had come from Victoria's Secret. My first thought was that David had a girlfriend living with him, and we would have to have a talk about it. Patty didn't really know what to do, so I thought maybe I would observe things for a bit.

I started seeing a pattern as to when the camisole would be put out on the line, and I thought I would try to catch David's friend on the compound. David, like many Kenyans, was a great cross-country runner and could run marathons down to the coast and back with no problem—and many times, without shoes. I realized that the pink camisole would always show up after his marathon runs on Saturdays. I asked him about the matter, and he said he loved to run in it because it felt "so good and cool." I laughed so hard that I cried, thinking about David running a marathon in a camisole. David never realized that the piece of clothing was intended for other purposes, and every time he would take off on a run wearing it, I would laugh and yell for Patty to come out and see.

The other memory so precious to us is when we would be cooking dinner and, without fail, David would come to the window and say, "Can you see me, Mama?" David said he was the "blackest African ever," so he could put his face up to the kitchen screen and you wouldn't see him. He was that dark, and we always laughed at his sense of humor during those surprise visits from him at the window.

Takeaway: In Africa, all things are recycled, especially clothing, which will be worn by men or women regardless of the color or texture.

BUYING A HOUSE ONLINE DURING A REVOLUTION

Do not plant a seed in the sea.

—*Swahili proverb*

On Monday morning after a long night of violence, I called the embassy, only to get a recorded voice message that said, "Call back Tuesday morning. The embassy is closed." The whole country had just melted down and was in freefall, and the American embassy was not open for business. It seemed strange to me, as I had been to the embassy before and thought they all stayed open, even during a revolution. That time was very different, and the situation on the ground was getting worse by the day.

On Tuesday morning, the embassy sent an email out that said they'd put together a plan. They suggested that we go to the airport; board a plane that would take us to Rabat, Morocco; and after that, we would have to find a way to continue to our next destination. They gave no info about how we would pay for the trip. They also said I wasn't even allowed to pull my car into the embassy parking lot. I was told to leave it outside.

I was in the process of transitioning my family back to the US so my children could return to high school, and I was considering buying a house in my hometown. The embassy was closed, but I needed a signed document I could only get from the American embassy. I decided to go to the embassy just in case someone was around. I got lucky and found a young lady packing up things inside the office. I knocked on the window because clearly nobody was around. Most Americans had evacuated the country and were heading home.

As I knocked louder, a person finally appeared in front of the window. I immediately showed her my form that I needed to have filled out, and she said through the thick glass, "We are closed." I showed her my passport and yelled that all I needed was a stamp from Tunisia that would validate my address and help me close on the house back in the States. She reluctantly grabbed the paper and searched around in a drawer for the right stamp. After an hour, she finally stamped it.

As I walked out of an unattended door, the whole place was having a meltdown, and I went back in to the population and a revolution. We eventually completed the process and bought the house, but we

TAKEAWAYS FROM THE AFRICAN CONTINENT

always laughed about the whole process with no embassy available to help us move forward with our paperwork and documents.

Takeaway: When all else fails, remind yourself of your mother's teaching that you can do anything you put your mind to, even with no American embassy around.

FISHING AND EATING WITH YOUR HANDS

If you find no fish, you have to eat bread alone.

—Ghanaian proverb

I fished in many places around the world, but Africa, by far, has the people who are best at catching fish by hand. One time, Patty and I were out on a small fishing boat which departed from a small island called Lamu near northern Mombasa, close to Somalia. We organized a fishing trip with some local guys from town, but we noticed that the guides had no fishing poles. I thought, *How can we be going fishing without a way to catch fish?* To my surprise, after we made it to the middle of the sea, the guides had fishing line wrapped around Styrofoam and small metal hooks that they had fashioned out of lead. I'm still not sure if they had the fish already hooked on the line and were just recatching them because we were expected to have a fish fry, but it was fun to fish that way in an old ancient boat.

Another funny fishing experience occurred during my time in North Africa. Just like in Kenya, we went out into the smooth waters, and the guides knew exactly where to go to catch fish. As in Kenya, they preferred to fish with their hands and did not have poles to fish with like me. But as we began to fish, they were outcatching me five to one on every cast. They had smaller hooks and knew the style and techniques to fish that way.

During our outing, many of the guys I was fishing with were Muslim, and they never missed a call to prayer. I was thinking they would surely miss it that time, as there was no room on the boat for them to go up and down as they prayed. Well, 9:00 p.m. hit, and you could clearly hear the call to prayer out on the water. The guys I was fishing with started praying, and I continued to fish. As they prayed, the boat was rocking up and down, which caused more action to the bait I was using, and I began to catch many more fish. I'm sure they realized what was going on, as I was throwing fish into the basket as fast as I could. When they stopped praying, the fish slowed down, and things went back to normal for me, but that had been a nice surprise out on the water on a beautiful summer night in Bizerte, Tunisia.

I'll never forget the first time I sat down at a restaurant and realized we would be eating with our hands; there were no eating utensils around. I was in Kenya's capital city, Nairobi, at an Ethiopian restaurant. The friends I was with had ordered a dish called *injira*, which is a typical dish from Ethiopia. It looks like a big, round disk with two eggs in the middle and has the texture of an ace bandage. The food was served on a small table, where everybody sat around the plate and all the other dishes were dumped onto it. You had to tear off a piece of bread to scoop up the food, which was quite an ordeal with five or so people eating at the same time.

Takeaway: Always be ready to change your life strategies to create new possibilities to catch more opportunities with your hands.

BROKEN LAWNMOWERS AND TOILET SEATS

Water is colorless and tasteless, but you can live on it longer than you can eating food.

—*African proverb*

Mombasa, Kenya, was diverse, from having an Indian population to the Africans. We worked at a school located on the island, right in the middle of everything that was going on in the city center. The school, over the years, would hire teachers from the States, who would bring in different ideas about how things should be done in terms of the property of the school buildings.

The first thing I noticed when I went on campus was a large pile of lawnmowers that had been thrown over in the corner. When I first went to investigate all the equipment, it seemed to be new and in good shape. I thought there had to be more going on with the situation. I noticed how the grass was being cut, and it dawned on me that, for one, the grass was very thick and most of the lawnmowers' blades struggled with the thickness off the grass and needed to be sharpened. That was one cause of the problem, and the other problem was that many of the students seemed to always be cutting grass for some reason.

I enquired more about it and came to realize that cutting grass in the schoolyard by hand was punishment given by some teachers to students who violated school dress codes or didn't do homework assignments. The lawnmowers, when they worked, required gas, which cost money. The most important thing was the student and worker were able to cut the grass too fast, which caused a problem—and you never do anything in Africa in a fast way.

That totally answered my question as to why those time-saving lawnmowers weren't being repaired and were viewed as more of an inconvenience rather than helpful. I never thought about that concept very much until I lived in Africa. There, time is not money, as we're taught here in the States. The other factor in the demise of the machines was that nobody had been taught to fix or maintain them, either.

Another ongoing issue at the school was broken toilet seats. I never thought that would be such a big problem. It always happened when a new headmaster would come to the school from the States. The teachers told me that they wouldn't put seats on the toilets because the seats would just get broken. The Americans could never figure that out. After a few days on the campus, I came to understand that the students had grown up squatting outside to go to the bathroom. Come to find out, the students and parents were squatting on top of the toilets instead of squatting on the ground. To fix the problem, the school needed to leave off the toilet seats or go back to the hole-in-the-ground type of bathroom.

Takeaway: Never impose your ways of doing things onto people or situations without first understanding the culture and thoughts of those involved.

THE CITY OF AL-QAEDA AND A MARRIAGE RETREAT

Do not light a fire under a fruit-bearing tree.

—Ghanaian proverb

This story is probably one of the most dangerous and crazy things I have done in my travels during my time living overseas. The company that we worked for many times would ask us to travel to lead marriage retreats since we had the privilege of receiving the training to do so. For this particular trip, we were asked to travel to the country of Yemen. Coming from North Africa, that was a culture shock, to say the least.

After we arrived in Sanaa, we were picked up at the airport by a former military gentleman and his wife, who volunteered to drive us all the way up to the small town of Tiese in the northern part of the country. We had to go to a guesthouse to rest up before we went on the long ride traversing some very dangerous roads. Coming from Tunisia, we had never seen women's faces completely covered. One of the most amazing things we witnessed was women eating fried chicken from a restaurant while still wearing the veil.

After the family had rested, we started on the long ride up to Tiese. An hour outside of town, my friend Ted decided we needed to get something to eat and pulled over to a roadside café. As I entered the restaurant, I noticed about thirty or so AK-47 guns lined up against the wall. All the men were eating quietly as their guns rested nearby. As I ordered our food, the surprising thing that occurred to me was that each man somehow knew which gun belonged to him.

On our way back from the retreat, we were followed by a small truck that had a 50-caliber gun mounted on the top of it. The truck was always right behind us. I wasn't really sure what was actually happening, but Ted didn't seem worried, so we just kept our heads down and acted like everything was normal. On our way back to the capital, my friend decided we needed to buy something in the town of Al-Qaeda. Ted told me that he would park the van outside a shop so we could run in and get some of the famous cloth from one of the shop owners, but that he would keep the van running in case something happened. We made a dash for it, and so I bought two beautiful pieces of cloth, traditional wraps worn around the waist for when you get out of the shower, from probably the most dangerous town in the world.

We eventually made it back down to the capital and prepared to leave to go to the airport. The airport in Yemen is one of the most bizarre places I have ever seen. As we were going through the metal detectors, men had their guns and knives spread out on the scanners, thinking it would be okay to sit with them on the plane. The airport attendant had to explain to them that they would have to leave their weapons and they would be sure to put them underneath the plane. There was such a commotion about this that the whole line was held up for quite some time, and a fight almost broke out. We eventually made it out and back to Egypt and then on to North Africa, very grateful to have lived to talk about it.

Takeaway: Never try to board a plane carrying things that will not go through the metal detector and then act like you don't know what the problem could be.

Made in the USA
Middletown, DE
12 January 2019